50 *Years of* sports Report

Sports Report has always been a team effort, and this book is no exception. Thanks to everyone in the BBC Radio Sportsroom for their advice and encouragement; to Tom Whiting and his colleagues at Collins Willow for their expertise and sang froid in the face of mounting deadlines; and to Christopher Pick for reviewing the text and making some valuable suggestions.

B B C RADIO 5 LIVE

50 *Years of* sports Report

INTRODUCED BY
DESMOND LYNAM

EDITED BY
AUDREY ADAMS

CollinsWillow
An Imprint of HarperCollins*Publishers*

First published in 1997 by CollinsWillow
an imprint of HarperCollins*Publishers*
London

© British Broadcasting Corporation 1997

1 3 5 7 9 8 6 4 2

A CIP catalogue record for this book is
available from the British Library

ISBN 0 00 218806 6

Photographs supplied courtesy of Allsport Photographic,
the BBC, Phil Sheldon and Peter Slater

Text design by Mick Sanders

Origination by Dot Gradations, Essex, UK

Printed and bound in Great Britain by Creative Print and Design,
Ebbw Vale, Blaenau, Gwent, Wales

The article *How It All Began* by Angus Mackay has been
reproduced with permission from William Heinemann publishers

CONTENTS

50th Birthday Greetings from...

Lord Cowdrey of Tonbridge

During the 1950s, I was invited to the *Sports Report* studio on several occasions to be 'grilled' (very lightly!) by Eamonn Andrews. One used to meet so many interesting people on these occasions – Peter Wilson, Raymond Glendenning, Max Robertson, Rex Alston, Harry Carpenter and of course John Arlott.

Angus Mackay, the producer, became a good friend. I remember we used to laugh about a letter my father, Ernest Cowdrey, wrote to the programme when it first started. He was a tea planter in Southern India and a keen cricketer, and he used to listen to *Sports Report* via the General Overseas Service of the BBC. He wrote to put my name forward as a promising cricketer of the future: I was still at school at the time, so I fear this was based on little more than parental optimism.

Still, 50 years on, Angus's sporting vision of the future has certainly proved to be well founded. Congratulations on the first half century – now for the next 50!

Henry Cooper OBE

I have fond memories of *Sports Report*, because I always used to regard it as my lucky programme. Back in the 1960s, when I had a fight coming up, Angus Mackay used to invite my manager Jim Wicks and me to the studio the previous Saturday to talk to

Eamonn Andrews. Of course Eamonn knew his stuff – he was an Irish amateur champion and often commentated on my fights as well. We boxers are a superstitious lot, we like to keep to the same routine, and I always seemed to win if I'd been on *Sports Report*.

I also used to tune in for the football results, especially my team Arsenal. My surgeon was the club doctor there, and I remember training with the Arsenal boys when I was getting over a cartilage operation. My world title fight against Muhammad Ali in 1966 was staged at Highbury too, but that was one time my luck ran out!

Best wishes to *Sports Report* on its 50th birthday, and lots of luck for the future!

Sir Bobby Charlton CBE

I've lived with *Sports Report* for as long as I can remember. When I was a boy, years before I joined Manchester United, tuning in at 5 o'clock was a regular Saturday ritual. That music would get the adrenalin going, and then we'd listen to all the results, followed by the match reports from the various grounds. It was compulsive, magical, and Saturdays weren't complete without it.

I was always so impressed by the eloquence of the reports. I particularly remember Geoffrey Green talking about the demise of Newcastle United when they were relegated from the first division – 1961, it must have been. It was like listening to poetry, and I was almost moved to tears.

These days, of course, you can also get the football results on television, but radio offers something extra: it exercises the imagination, and it still gives me as big a thrill to listen as when I was a child. *Sports Report* and I have grown up together and I have great pleasure in wishing the programme a very Happy Birthday.

Gareth Edwards MBE

I will always remember the back kitchen of my parents' home in the Welsh-speaking village of Gwaen-cae-Gurwen. There was a brown, wooden wireless, our link with the world outside via the Welsh Home Service and the Light Programme. It was my father's pride and joy and it had a sort of luminous eye near the top which glowed so bright when the room was dark on long winter evenings.

Having played football and rugby on Saturday mornings and afternoons, we would rush home in time for *Sports Report* and the sound of the signature tune, and then the mid-Atlantic voice of Eamonn Andrews with the football results. Swansea Town – as they were in those days – were my favourite team. I almost signed professional forms for them years later, but rugby won the day. When Wales were playing away from home, we snuggled around the set in the hope of hearing G. V. Wynne-Jones and Rex Alston report a Welsh victory.

When I eventually played for Wales and the British Lions I was interviewed for the programme, and I particularly remember Peter Jones, the presenter then, because he came from Swansea. I knew that my mother and father would be listening, for *Sports Report* was a must for our family. The wireless brought sport alive, long before television had arrived. We clung to every word and then rushed outside and pretended to be one of the afternoon's heroes.

I actually met Eamonn Andrews when he introduced my *This Is Your Life* programme, and I told him of the early days when we listened to *Sports Report* in our back kitchen more than forty years ago. 'It was my favourite programme, not to be missed on Saturdays,' I said. 'Mine too,' said Eamonn.

Yes, *Sports Report* will always be important to me just like the sweet, wild honey of the Mabinogion.

Sebastian Coe OBE

One of the most evocative sounds in sport for me is the *Sports Report* five o'clock signature tune – 'Out of the Blue'. It heralds the classified football results, that moment of truth for all committed supporters. There was a period in the mid-1970s when I went two whole seasons without missing a single Chelsea away match. We'd make our way out of some northern outpost and rush to the car, anxious to learn whether the two points we'd just picked up at Bolton or wherever would be enough to save Chelsea from relegation for another year (we just about held on!).

Sport on radio has always been and still is an integral part of my life – especially on long car journeys. I can remember driving back from athletics meetings in the UK and listening to reports on our own performances – a chastening experience! Nowadays I can spend two or three hours in the car and become completely wrapped up in the commentary on a football match which I wouldn't bother with on television. That's the great quality of radio: it has an intimacy and an immediacy that makes it so much more exciting and involving for the audience. *Sports Report* has been in the vanguard of all that's good about sports broadcasting in this country for 50 years and long may it continue.

MAGIC MOMENTS...

Commentators can be embarrassed by what they say on the air in the heat of the moment, but during a Cup tie at the Baseball Ground, Alan Green suffered embarrassment of a different kind.

He was in full flow during the second half when a tannoy announcement asked the owner of a silver Peugeot to return to his car in the car park because it was making a high-pitched whining noise. A sheepish commentator had to admit on the air that the car in question was his. Rumours that Alan had left the radio on can be discounted. He had to hand over commentary to Jon Champion to return to his ailing car. As it turned out, nothing was seriously wrong with it, and when Alan returned to the commentary box he was not amused.

DESMOND LYNAM

Introduction

'You wouldn't knock down Tower Bridge and replace it with some monstrous reinforced concrete edifice simply because it's old fashioned, would you? No, well, don't tamper with this. It's part of the fabric of sports broadcasting. It's a tradition.' Well, it went something like that. It was my impassioned plea to the management of the BBC Radio sports department to keep faith with 'Out of the Blue', the signature tune synonymous with radio sport which you can still hear each Saturday at five o'clock.

They had been thinking of 'updating' it. Changing it for something more 'modern'. Thankfully my strange analogy did not fall on deaf ears, and *De Dum De Dum De Dum De Dum Diddly Dum De Dum* goes on.

That all happened back in the 1970s. I had first listened to *Sports Report* in the 1950s. Eamonn Andrews was the presenter, his mellifluous voice a sea of calm as he led you north and south and to Scotland for those urgent stories from White Hart Lane and Old Trafford and Ibrox. Then magically he would be joined 'live' from New York by Peter Wilson of the *Daily Mirror* reporting on the build-up to the latest world heavyweight title fight. The line would often break, adding to the fascination of even the possibility of this inter-continental communication.

I was enthralled each fortnight. Fortnight? Well, every other Saturday I was watching Brighton and Hove Albion. So it was only on 'away match' days that I was glued to the bakelite set in our living room for the *Five O'Clock Show*. You see, in those days we didn't have a car radio. In fact we didn't have a car.

Not in my wildest dreams could I have imagined in those short-trousered, grey-flannelled days that, not so many years on, I would actually be sitting in Eamonn's chair. Sadly less calm and certainly nowhere near as honey-toned as the great man. The other great man was, however, still very much present when I arrived.

Angus. Angus Mackay, whose very idea the whole programme had been, was still at the helm. Or rather at the ear. Angus produced the programme, as he had right from the start, sitting next to the presenter in the live studio. His production instructions were delivered in urgent whispers, not all of them heard at the first attempt. To say that this led to moments of unease would be like saying that at times Paul Gascoigne has been a little silly.

Our partnership just about survived two years, during which Angus probably rued the day that television had taken Eamonn away from him. Then he went off to enjoy a long and happy retirement. The only praise I ever got from Angus came after about twenty or so programmes together. On the way up in the lift from studio B9 in the basement of Broadcasting House, he said to me 'Not bad, old son, not bad'. I sailed off into what was left of the weekend like a giddy teenager. This was praise indeed.

Many years later, I met Angus again, at a reunion party. By now I had been in television for some time. In his late seventies by now, Angus strode up to me. I was expecting the worst. 'Just keep doing it like you're doing it, old son,' he said. 'But watch out for those split infinitives.' Another onset of teenage giddiness.

Angus's successor Bob Burrows and a whole list of outstanding producers and presenters who have followed have kept *Sports Report* right at the top of broadcast sports journalism. I am so proud to be an 'old boy' and to have played a small part in an ongoing story which has now lasted a half-century. In broadcasting terms, we're talking Tower Bridge.

ANGUS MACKAY

How It All Began

Angus Mackay was the founding producer of
Sports Report: *a formidable Scot who demanded*
the highest standards, both journalistic and
technical. He was associated with the programme
for 24 years until his retirement in 1972. In 1954
he and Eamonn Andrews edited the very first
Sports Report *book (published by Heinemann),*
from which this extract is taken.

The only way one can appreciate the stress and strain, the high
tension created in the production of *Sports Report* is to see the
programme go out from the studio. Most BBC producers are
given ample time to rehearse and prepare their programmes,
but on the other hand *Sports Report* goes out so soon after the
end of the day's sport that, far from having a complete
rehearsal, we are usually working from hand to mouth while it
is being broadcast

Imagine, if you will, a large room, say 30 feet long by 18 feet
wide, divided centrally by a glass partition. One half is the
studio and the other houses all the special, elaborate
engineering equipment necessary for the production of *Sports
Report*, which on occasions has brought in reports from no
fewer than 15 towns up and down the country within the space
of 30 minutes. Here sit the producer, his secretary and the
engineers (the backbone of every programme) who control all
incoming and outgoing contributions and records being used in

the programme. There is a loudspeaker in both halves through which instructions are pouring out to reporters up and down the country and which relay back to us suggestions and acknowledgement of the general briefing. On top of this we may have an engineer editing or timing the recording of a race commentary, while on either side of the glass partition you may find Fleet Street columnists or such personalities in sport as Sir Stanley Rous, Freddie Mills, Bobby Locke, Jack Solomons, or maybe some famous American boxer working out points with me or with each other regarding the coming broadcast. It seems all are talking at once and no one is listening to anyone else.

A visitor to the studio would find this bedlam starting off at five o'clock and mounting steeply to an almost unbearable pitch until, at about five seconds to half-past five, and without any audible signal there is an electrifying silence, which even now, after 17 years with the BBC, still starts the 'butterflies' going in the Mackay stomach. This is the moment when we cross our fingers, pray that all instructions have been received clearly by the people taking part, and that the last piece of this intangible jigsaw has dropped into place. The red light flicks, becomes steady, and yet another edition of *Sports Report* is launched.

Up to 1939 we hadn't been allowed to put out any sports news before 6.15pm, and the inauguration of *Sports Report* on 3 January 1948 offered new fields to explore and profit by; risks to be met and taken; above all something new – something with the taste of adventure to it. Being one of those contradictions in terms, an incautious Scot, I accepted the brief immediately.

Even the choice of the signature tune was not without its excitement. For several weary days we had been listening to literally dozens of gramophone records trying to find a suitable melody. It seemed that we had exhausted the reserves of the gramophone library, and we were not very happy about the disc we had chosen when, in the late afternoon of our first broadcast, the library came through to say that there were a few more discs available if we had time to hear them. We did find time that afternoon, and one of the first we heard was a march called 'Out of the Blue' composed by Hubert Bath. This was just what we had been looking for and almost immediately it was whisked up to the studio, slapped on the turntable and used to introduce the first edition. Since then 'Out of the Blue' has been broadcast in many programmes and even now, though *Sports Report* has been running about six years, we still receive letters asking for the title, and information as to where sheet music and gramophone records can be bought.

I often look back on the early editions of *Sports Report* with some amusement. In 1948, we used to think we were putting on fast, slick shows, but if we could compare them with those of today we would probably find as wide a difference as there is between the Spitfire and the Hawker-Hunter.

In those days we used to give as much as two and a half minutes to a report on a soccer match, and we got what we deserved – flowery, well-padded stories which contained a good deal of wholly unnecessary information. We learned the hard way because there was no precedent for a programme such as this, but it wasn't long before we realised that a good radio reporter could give us an accurate, informative picture of a game in something like a minute and a quarter or a minute and a half. Even today our carefully chosen team of football reporters grumble that they cannot adequately cover a game within these limits of time, but the fact that they can and do produce good reports doesn't help their argument.

In organising our coverage of matches for any one Saturday we first select the most important or attractive games and then go into ways and means of having reports on them. This second point is the more important because, owing to the early hour at which the programme goes on the air, we have to study very carefully the locality of the grounds we have chosen in relation to the BBC studios in order to get our reporters there in time for the broadcast. Our main centres are, of course, Plymouth, Bristol, Southampton, London, Birmingham, Cardiff, Swansea, Sheffield, Manchester, Leeds, Newcastle, Glasgow and Edinburgh. There are also small auxiliary studios elsewhere, but these are not always available to us when we need them. Unfortunately, we have a few blind spots which prevent us from covering home games played by some important clubs, much to the fury of the supporters concerned. Examples are Stoke, Preston, Derby and Middlesbrough.

It is true that in the middle of the season, when the matches finish early in the afternoon, we can go further afield, but for the other two-thirds – the beginning and the end of the season – life becomes very difficult indeed for our reporters. For example, a match starting at 3.15pm will end probably somewhere about five minutes to five, so just put yourself in the shoes of the unhappy reporter who is out, say, at White Hart Lane, the ground of Tottenham Hotspur. He has got little more than half an hour in which to get out of the ground and make a nine-mile journey through the busy streets of London to Broadcasting House. He travels by car, but even so must reach Studio 4A with a clear, precise account of the match which might be put on the air as early as 5.35pm. But wherever our reporters go they invariably find the club managers ready and willing to help in any way they can; while on big match day – such as cup-ties – the police often help us out with special parking facilities.

Now, I'm prepared to agree that the results and reports on the big soccer games attract a good proportion of the huge audience which listens to *Sports Report* on Saturday evenings, but I must confess that for my own part I get more satisfaction and fun out of the Talking Sport section, which has been a feature of the programme these past few years. Here, we try to present the listener not only with the very latest news from the world of sport, but also expert comment and opinion either on the outcome of such news or the background to it. This is a feature which calls for broadcasters who have a first-class working knowledge of most sports; flexible minds which can adapt themselves quickly to the ebb and flow of radio discussions; and above all, absolute reliability, trustworthiness at the microphone. This last point I would place first in importance because all discussions in *Sports Report* are carried through without script or rehearsal. It is our aim to be absolutely up-to-the-minute with our views on topics of the moment in the world of sport, and this we could not achieve without having readily available a team of experts to comment on or give their views about any story flashed to us by the news agencies, even on the day of broadcast. Very often we do not decide the topic until perhaps lunch-time Saturday, and on some occasions we have altered the subject not many minutes before going on the air.

In these discussions there is a very important person who should have been mentioned before now, and that is the narrator. In fact, I would go further and say that the narrator is THE key to the whole programme. On the surface it is a straight-forward job. He merely introduces each speaker and then takes the chair for the round-table discussion. It looks just as easy as that, but believe me it is anything but. I've come across only three men during the six-year run of *Sports Report* who have everything plus. They are Stewart McPherson and Raymond Glendenning, both leading sports commentators before *Sports Report* was ever thought of, and Eamonn Andrews, who appeared out of the blue after the start of the programme. Our first meeting came about purely by chance. It happened one evening that I heard *Ignorance is Bliss* [a comedy quiz programme introduced by Eamonn Andrews] and was rather impressed by the voice and radio personality of this newcomer from Ireland. A couple of months later a colleague brought Eamonn into our club, and after speaking to him for only a minute or two I made a quick decision which I have never since regretted. At the end of that week he was introducing a programme very similar to *Sports Report* but which is broadcast only in the General Overseas Service of the BBC; at the end of it I knew I was 'on a winner' and offered to put him on *Sports Report* in the Light Programme immediately, provided he was prepared to give me an option on his services as far as Saturdays were concerned. He was, and from there we have never looked back.

Yes, we have the experts, the technicians and a great team spirit. But behind it all lies the unblinking, ever-prominent face of the clock in Studio 4A, reminding us Saturday nights that we have just thirty minutes in which to tell our story. Passively suggesting, too, I sometimes think, that a move from 5.30 to 6pm would make life so much easier for everyone concerned. But suppose we were offered and accepted that half-hour's grace; it would no longer be *Sports Report*, would it?

BRYON BUTLER

1948: The Way it Was

*Owner of one of the most distinctive Radio
voices, Bryon Butler was the BBC's Football
Correspondent for over 20 years. The author of
definitive histories of the Football Association
and the FA Cup, Bryon is a keen cricketer who
has taken over 500 wickets in club matches.*

Nineteen-forty-eight; and *Sports Report* was created on the
third day. Its birth caused few quakes on earth but it must have
been noticed in the penthouse suite of Mount Olympus because
the year which followed was full of sublime sporting theatre –
an *annus mirabilis*, heaven-sent, to mark the first tottery steps
of a broadcasting phenomenon.

Britain was still frayed and shaken by a war it had won, and
ration books still mattered more than any written by
Shakespeare, but sport helped provide the promise of a better
tomorrow in one heady and irresistible package. Queues
wrapped themselves around football and cricket grounds like
endless woollen scarves. People wanted excitement and
normality, and sport answered the call. And so did *Sports
Report* whose audience would rise to 12 million before
television became something more than a minor peep-show.

Sports Report's timing, in any case, has always been
impeccable. Angus Mackay, its Godfather, had a stop-watch
where other mortals had a heart; and the programme's kick-off
at the start of such a sovereign year must not be regarded as a

simple coincidence. *Sports Report* was born on a peak, but some things are meant to be.

The year bristled with events, moments and names which even now, half a century on, ring clarion bells. The London Olympics were a surpassing success. Australia's greatest party of cricketers, led by an immortal, came and conquered imperiously. England's footballers were assuredly second to none. The 1948 FA Cup final was one of the tournament's finest. Britain was on the high plateau, too, in golf, boxing and even cycling; and Gordon Richards became champion jockey for the 21st time while a 12-year-old called Lester Piggott won his first race in a selling handicap at Haydock Park.

But, above all, the XIVth Olympiad: London's own and the first to be staged since Hitler's propaganda Games in Berlin in 1936. Britain didn't strike gold in the athletics, though there were winners on water, in the rowing and yachting, and a respectable sprinkling of silver. Nothing much more was realistically expected. British athletics was run by pernickety gentlemen of the old school, donations were heavily restricted and advertisements involving individuals were forbidden. Britain's success, however, was the paramount one: the hosting of the Games.

It was an act of courage, faith and even madness to apply for the Games; and their success was a triumph for common sense and hard labour. All this against a grey-glum backcloth of blitzed streets, breadline wages and stern rationing. There were restrictions on coal and gas, and on wintry mornings the nation peered through window panes made beautiful by filigree images in hoar-frost of ferns and trees. Motorists were even rationed to 90 miles a month for a while, though a car parked outside was the swankiest of status symbols. An Austin A40 Dorset ('something really new and thrilling') cost £315 plus £88 purchase tax to get on the road. Craven 'A' cigarettes ('for your throat's sake') came a little cheaper at 1s 4d (7 pence) for ten. A pint of beer cost the same.

The overall state of the nation was poorly, and during the year before the Games the Labour Prime Minister Clem Attlee called for 'sacrifice akin to war'. He spoke of 'peril and anxiety' and said he had 'no easy word for the people'. 'Work or Want' was one of many depressing official slogans. Naturally, too, there were professional tub-thumpers in Westminster and Fleet Street who railed against the whole notion of hosting the Games. Wrong place, wrong time etc. They did not begin to understand the value of sport as a moral and physical pick-me-up.

These were the 'Austerity Games' and every expense possible was spared. Familiar old venues were used, Wembley, the Empire Pool, Bisley, Herne Hill, Henley and so on, and with ingenuity, sweat and a bit of help their overhaul was completed on time. Finland and Sweden sent thousands of planks of wood for use at Wembley, chartering boats just for the purpose. And the British public also rose to the occasion: the Wembley box-office often had to stay open until midnight. A series ticket for the eight days of athletics cost £16 16s (£16.80), more than a fortnight's wages for the average working man, but they all sold.

Wembley's full houses rose, above all, to two of the 5,000 athletes from 59 countries who took part: Emil Zatopek of Czechoslovakia, with his grimacing face and rolling gait, and Fanny Blankers-Koen, a 30-year-old Dutch housewife. Zatopek won the 10,000 metres by nearly a full lap, looking as if every stride was going to be his last, and this son of a poor carpenter left no one in doubt that he was one of the finest distance runners of all time. He went on to break every world record from 5,000 to 30,000 metres, and in the 1952 Olympics in Helsinki he won the 5,000 metres, 10,000 metres and the marathon, a unique treble.

But it was the blonde Dutch housewife, a mother of two children, who dominated the London Olympics. Fanny Blankers-Koen won four gold medals, in the 80 metres hurdles, 100 metres, 200 metres and 4 x 100 relay, breaking two Olympic records along the way and wowing the world with her charm and modesty. She was even forgiven for beating three British girls, Maureen Gardner, Dorothy Manley and Audrey Williamson, into second place in her three individual events. She then returned to Amsterdam to receive a gift from her neighbours – a bicycle.

There was one sport, however, at which the English knew they were best. They had 'invented' football nearly a hundred years before, and nothing much had happened in the meantime to convince them anyone could play it better. There were embarrassments ahead, defeat by the United States in the 1950 World Cup and then by Hungary at Wembley in 1953, but the events of 1948 only sustained the lofty conviction that English football had no peer.

Walter Winterbottom, a tall, personable and scholarly man, a former Manchester United wing-half and RAF wing-commander, was England's manager – and he had so much talent to conjure with that English football's patriarchal airs and graces were almost forgivable. England played six games in 1948, won five, drew one, 19 goals scored, two conceded, and did it all with a swagger. They scored six against Northern Ireland, and also against Switzerland, but the high-point of the year came in Turin in May.

Italy had won the previous World Cup, in France in 1938, and their combative and virile side was still rated (outside England) as the finest in the world. But England beat them by 4–0 with such stylish conviction that shop windows in Turin displayed pictures of Winterbottom's team which read simply: Made in Britain. England's forwards that day were the 'Wizard of Dribble', the 'Blackpool Bombshell', the 'finest centre-forward ever to play for England', the 'Golden Boy of Soccer', and the 'Preston Plumber' – otherwise known as Stanley Matthews, Stan Mortensen, Tommy Lawton, Wilf Mannion and Tom Finney who later wrote: 'That performance was the greatest by any team I played for.'

The famous victory in Turin followed 'Wembley's finest final'; and the nation had the word on that of the *News of the World* which described Manchester United's 4–2 victory over Blackpool as 'a game that will leave an imperishable memory with all who saw it, a classic exhibition'. Mortensen and Matthews, who had just been voted the first Footballer of the Year, were in coruscating form and Blackpool led by 2–1 with only 20 minutes to go. But United, managed by Matt Busby and captained by the immaculate Johnny Carey, then scored three times to win their first final since 1909. The triumph was hugely deserved because United were then playing at Maine Road (Old Trafford had been flattened by bombs) and had overcome a First Division club in every round on the way to Wembley.

It was estimated that about a third of the nation listened to Raymond Glendenning's radio commentary on the final. Glendenning, a broad-based chap with a handlebar moustache, was a national celebrity whose clear, staccato voice conveyed the atmosphere and drama of the game with arresting effect. He was the first man to introduce *Sports Report*, but he was not a willing studio man. He was at his best when he had a front seat at one of the country's major sporting events. He had the precious gift of being able to make his listeners feel they were sitting next to him. BBC Television claimed an audience of one million, but this was wishful thinking. The official number of licences in force was fewer than 35,000 – which meant, according to the Beeb's figures, that 28 people watched the game on each set.

Arsenal won the Football League championship in resounding fashion, leading from the start to finish and clinching their sixth title with nearly a month to spare. Their 'retreating' defence conceded only 32 goals, and some thought they were boring, but in truth they were a balanced and aggressive side who scored the same number of goals (81) as runners-up Manchester United. Arsenal were led by 33-year-old Joe Mercer, once of Everton and England, whose wonderful smile and corkscrew legs endeared him to most people. Their only real set-back was a third round defeat in the FA Cup by Bradford Park Avenue whose centre-half was a determined chap called Ron Greenwood.

Sporting Britain loved it all. The total League attendance for season 1947-48 soared past 40 million for the first time and a record 83,260 squeezed into Maine Road to watch Manchester United draw with Arsenal. An average home crowd of more than 56,000 saw Newcastle win promotion from the Second Division, and 143,470 witnessed the Scottish Cup semi-final between Glasgow Rangers and Hibernian at Hampden Park. The 1948 FA Cup final was played, incidentally, in late April, alongside a full League programme, and attendances fell starkly by a third to less than 700,000. The absentees were listening to the broadcast from Wembley! The Cup, then, counted for more than the League. But the trend was upwards and the aggregate League attendance for 1948-49 rose to an all-time high of 41,271,414.

Cricket, when its turn came, matched football all the way for character and variety, though England found the going painfully bumpy. Not even the divine likes of Len Hutton, Cyril Washbrook, Bill Edrich, Alec Bedser, Godfrey Evans and the irrepressible Denis Compton (every schoolboy's hero and a man who even found time to help Arsenal win the League title) could make any sort of impression on Don Bradman's Australians. The tourists won four of the five Tests and dismissed England for 52 (Ray Lindwall 6 for 20) in the final meeting at the Oval.

It was Bradman's last tour and everyone wanted to see the greatest butcher of bowling the game has known. Alongside him were other men from the Pantheon of the game, Lindwall, the dashing Keith Miller, Lindsay Hassett, Sid Barnes and Bill Johnston among them, but the Don was the star attraction. He was given a thunderous reception when he walked out at the Oval to bat for the last time in a Test match. He needed just four runs to finish with a Test average of 100 – and was promptly bowled for nought, second ball, by a googly from Eric Hollies. It was suggested that he was so touched by his reception that he couldn't see the ball because of tears in his eyes. 'A great exaggeration', he insisted in later years. 'It was a perfect ball which deceived me.' But he did admit the ovation moved him deeply and made him anxious.

The Australians summarily demolished most of the county sides, and scored 721 on one balmy Saturday against Essex at Southend, still a record, before dismissing their opponents twice in a day. Glamorgan, led with fire and iron by Wilf Wooller, won the county championship for the first time; but English cricket knew in its heart it was second best. The Don said farewell with an average for the summer of nearly 90 and 11 centuries – including one in each of his last three games.

Joe Louis, the 'Brown Bomber', the king of heavyweights, ruled the world of boxing; and, a few inches and pounds down the scale, Rinty Monaghan of Belfast knocked out Jackie Paterson to become world flyweight champion. But England's favourite ring-master was Freddie Mills, a rugged lion with a mane of dark hair and an ear-to-ear smile, who beat America's Gus Lesnevich on points in a classic return at the White City to win the world light heavyweight title.

Mills, who learnt his trade in an old-time fairground boxing booth, was a regular contributor to *Sports Report*; and so was Henry Cotton, a very different sort of fellow, who won the British Open golf championship for the third time. Here was the toughest of competitors. Nothing scratched his concentration. He was a Londoner who spoke his mind, and was sometimes misunderstood, but few men have done more for British golf. Reg Harris, moreover, did the same for cycling. Hindered by injuries, he managed 'only' two silver medals in the 1948 Olympics, but he then turned professional and won the world sprint title four times. Harris, whose mightily developed thighs looked like sections of an oak tree, was something of a hero in England but an idol on the continent: a real super-star.

There were, however, one or two things happening in Britain which had absolutely nothing to do with sport. The railways were nationalised on New Year's Day, electricity followed on April Fool's Day and the National Health Service ('from cradle to grave') came into being in early July.

King George VI and Queen Elizabeth celebrated their silver wedding; and their elder daughter, Princess Elizabeth, gave birth to a son, Charles Philip Arthur George. The Registrar General reported a boom in babies, a 21 per cent increase which was attributed to couples 'catching up' after the war years. The Aga Khan's My Love won the Derby and, later in the year, the Kinsey Report, an American study into the sexual behaviour of the human male, was a sensation.

These were such morally corseted times that the producers of *Dick Barton, Special Agent*, a cult serial, issued a dozen rules to ensure that their hero's lily-white character was never besmirched. They included 'sex plays no part in his adventures', 'no lies', 'no swearing' and a strict order that violence was restricted to 'clean socks on the jaw'.

The country also knew what it liked. There were queues at the cinemas for *Hamlet* (with Laurence Olivier) and *Treasure of the Sierra Madre*. 'On a Slow Boat to China' was a hit song. There was demand for Norman Mailer's first novel *The Naked and the Dead* and Evelyn Waugh's *The Loved One*. There was earnest discussion about Tennessee Williams' Pulitzer winning play *A Streetcar Named Desire*. And thousands had a jolly good time at Butlin holiday camps.

This was *Sports Report*'s new world; and on 3 January 1948 it duly took its Light Programme place in the tuppenny *Radio Times* between *BBC Variety Orchestra and Chorus with Denny Dennis* and at 6pm *Jazz Club*. Television was squeezed into a couple of pages at the back and in the morning papers its output was confined to just three lines. Television, on the face of things, did not have much of a future.

FRED TRUEMAN

Cricket in the 1950s: May and Laker

The archetypal England fast bowler, Frederick Sewards Trueman (aka 'Fiery Fred'), was the first cricketer to take 300 Test wickets, and took 100 wickets or more in ten consecutive seasons for Yorkshire. He remains a great character and raconteur and a regular summariser for Test Match Special.

The 1950s were a golden era for cricket in England. We still had established players like Len Hutton, Denis Compton and Bill Edrich from before the War – all great players – and Alec Bedser was still the best medium-fast bowler in the world. Then there were people like Brian Statham, Frank Tyson and myself coming through – Tony Lock, Johnny Wardle, Bob Appleyard, Jim Laker, the list is endless – and among the batsmen Peter May, Colin Cowdrey, Tom Graveney and Ken Barrington. The country had been through a bad time for six years and people were looking to the likes of Compton and Hutton for something special. That was in the days that county grounds were packed – especially for games involving the big boys, Surrey, Middlesex, Lancashire and of course Yorkshire – and if you didn't get to the ground by quarter to eleven on the first morning then you didn't get in at all. The novelty of Test cricket was still there too: nowadays Test cricket is like a travelling circus – they play Test cricket all the time and I'm afraid the sense of occasion is no longer there.

Among all the players I've mentioned, I'd single out Peter May as without doubt the greatest English player since the war. He was elegant and refined, but there was plenty of steel behind those boyish looks, especially when we were playing the Australians: he respected them of course but he always wanted to beat them. When he was batting, you'd always feel something would happen: he was a wonderful onside player and hit the ball very hard.

He captained England 41 times, and, without being disparaging, I thought he was lucky to have so many great players to call on, particularly in the bowling department where we tend to struggle today. He was a great guy as far as I was concerned. We came from very different backgrounds, but he was a nice man who treated everyone the same, and it turned out we had a great deal in common. We were both great competitors, both proud Englishmen, and we both wanted to win. Even if he wasn't captain, if you'd bowled well he'd come up and put his arm around your shoulder and say 'well bowled'. As skipper, he was never afraid to ask other players for advice, and take it. If things weren't working out we'd have a chat and try something else: if you know you've got your captain behind you, and the skipper knows he's got his bowler behind him, it rubs off and you both gain confidence.

I remember we were playing Surrey at the Oval in 1956. He said he had some bad news for me – that I'd been left out of the party to tour South Africa that winter. To be honest, I'd already guessed – I hadn't really expected to go. But he also promised it would be the last time I'd be left out, as he wanted me in the England side, and he was as good as his word. From 1957 to 1963 I generally took the new ball, and in 1964 I became the first man in history to take 300 Test wickets. Peter was one of the first people to congratulate me – even though he wasn't actually playing that day.

Another time we were playing the West Indies at Sabina Park, Jamaica. But for two very bad decisions by the West Indian umpire we'd have won the Test and I'd have come out with six or seven wickets – as it was, I got four bowling for a long time in extreme heat. Peter kept chatting to me to keep me going – 'Come on now, he said, 'England expects' – and I said 'Is that why they call it the mother country?' and he fell about laughing at that. We won the series 1–0, and Peter was delighted. He was one of the few people in authority whom you could sit and talk to. We became very friendly, and it was a friendship that carried on even after we'd both retired from the game. I never called him Peter, always PBH, and he called me FST.

I was playing at Edgbaston when he got his 285 against the West Indies in 1957 – one of his greatest innings. They were having trouble with Sonny Ramadin, who was a fantastic bowler – a mystery bowler they called him. He used to bowl like an off-spinner, but then he'd make one hold up and go the other way, like a leg cutter. I'd played against him for Yorkshire – I'd watched his hand and seen how he did it, and once I'd spotted it I didn't have any problem with him. So I had a word with Peter, and of course he went out and got 285 – Colin Cowdrey got 154 at the other end. I must admit we'd booked out of the hotel before that stand – it looked as though we'd had it – and we had to book back into the hotel on the Monday night. In the end we nearly won the game. That was the very first match covered by *Test Match Special* – little did I think that 40 years later I would be a big part of the programme. I've had a great time doing commentary with the radio team: I try to tell it as I see it even if it occasionally makes me unpopular, and I love humour – I've always found it easy to laugh and have a bit of fun.

Jim Laker was a fellow Yorkshireman, born in Frizinghall, near Bradford. His father was a stonemason, but I'm not sure Jim knew him very well: certainly Jim didn't know where he was buried until late in life. It was a strange business – my old mate Peter Parfitt, who played for Middlesex and England, used to have a country inn at Elslack in the Yorkshire Dales, and he found the grave in Barnoldswick churchyard. Naturally, he told Jim and took him there. Anyway, somehow Jim escaped the net and played nearly all his cricket down south for Surrey. There's a story that some Yorkshire people went down to see him in about 1948 to try to bring him back north – but by then he was settled in his bank job and said no. So he stayed with Surrey, and was one of the main reasons they won the Championship seven years on the trot from 1952 to 1958 – which is a most wonderful record.

I always got on very well with Jim, who was a fellow Aquarian. He was a wonderful spin bowler, and when he was bowling well you could hear the finger click. I used to stand close to the wicket, with great confidence – I never did get hit when he was bowling, and I took quite a few catches off him in Test cricket. He was a big spinner of the ball and very accurate – if he got on a wicket that helped him he would bowl you out. Of course the records he set were out of this world. He took ten wickets in an innings twice – 19 wickets in the match for England against Australia at Old Trafford in 1956 of course, and ten wickets for Surrey against the Australians at The Oval in the same season. Absolutely fantastic – though of course the Australians weren't great players of offspin bowling. The Aussies said it was all down to the conditions here, and he wouldn't dare to go to Australia. But in 1958 he did go over there, and he bowled superbly – the Australians still couldn't get him away. He went to the West Indies too, and he didn't get hammered round there either, even though the wickets were like tablecloths – wonderful batting wickets but not very good for bowlers.

A lot of people accused Jim of not liking it when the going got tough – whereas his counterpart Tony Lock would bowl until his fingers bled. It wasn't a description that applied as far as I was concerned – I just thought he was a world-class offspin bowler, one of the best of all time. He could make the ball float away from the right-handed batsman, he could spin it viciously, bowl the arm ball – he could bowl everything, and he could bat a bit as well. Jim was a quiet, private sort of person, but he had a very dry sense of humour and enjoyed a drink and a cigarette. I enjoyed playing with him and liked him very much indeed.

I didn't listen to the wireless too much when I was growing up in Yorkshire: I liked the country life, especially birdwatching, which is a hobby I still enjoy today. However I have one special memory of *Sports Report*. It was 15 August 1964 – a Saturday afternoon – and the Fifth Test against Australia at the Oval. My old mate Neil Hawke nicked a catch to Colin Cowdrey and that was my 300th Test wicket. Frank Nicklin, my editor at the *People*, had asked me if I could possibly take my 300th wicket on a Saturday afternoon. I'd told him things like that couldn't be done to order, but that it might happen – and it did. Anyway, I remember Peter West interviewing me for the programme while I was in the bath – we had our photo taken too. And Frank Nicklin sent me a case of vintage champagne.

MAGIC MOMENTS...

Reading the racing results in *Sports Report* often causes problems, as broadcasters grapple with unfamiliar or amusing names. During the week, the classified racing results are always recorded in an effort to retain a level of dignity and decorum. In *Sports Report*, they are read 'live' with presenters doing everything in their power to prevent the broadcaster's nightmare – the corpse.

Whipper's Delight, Roger the Butler and Lord Podgski have precipitated much mirth on the airwaves, as the Uncontrollable tries to master the Unpronounceable. In future, even if you haven't had a bet, listen out to hear whether the corpse can be kept 'underground'.

PETER BROMLEY

Fifty Years of Racing on the Radio

The BBC's first-ever sports correspondent, Peter Bromley has called home the winner of every Derby and Grand National since 1961 on BBC Radio. A former amateur rider and trainer, Peter has many other sporting interests, including motor-racing and shooting.

When *Sports Report* was unleashed on the public in January 1948, the timing for the introduction of an entirely new form of sports reportage was perfect. We were living in a time of bleak austerity, controls and high taxation. After the War years the nation had an insatiable appetite for sport and attendance at soccer and rugby matches, cricket and racing reached extraordinary levels. The public was equally hungry for sports stories. The new programme with its catchy signature tune was an instant success, giving not only the results but eye-witness accounts by some of the big names in Fleet Street within minutes of the final whistle. It was fast-moving, highly professional, and controlled by an articulate and knowledgeable link man in the studio. Those early programmes used Raymond Glendenning in the chair as well as Stewart Macpherson, the fast-talking Canadian who had made a name for himself as an ice hockey commentator, and later Eamonn Andrews, who had become well known as a boxing commentator, with his beguiling Irish brogue and unflappable style.

The BBC had always covered most major sports live by running commentaries in the Light Programme (later to become Radio Two). However this activity was under the control of the BBC's Entertainment Department and came under the banner of the BBC's Outside Broadcast Department whose Chief, S. J. de Lotbiniere (nicknamed Lobby and also known as 'HOBS', Head of Outside Broadcasts Sound), was the architect of the highly successful technique of delivering fast-moving descriptions of the play. In what was the golden age of radio, Raymond Glendenning became its most outstanding personality, switching from soccer to racing and boxing with consummate ease.

Other well known voices involved with broadcasting live sport were Brian Johnston, Rex Alston, Peter West and Max Robertson. They all became household names and were jealously guarded by HOBS.

The new programme, *Sports Report*, came under News Division and was entirely separate from the Outside Broadcast Department. This strange arrangement was soon to develop into tension between the strong personality of Angus Mackay, Editor of *Sports Report*, and Charles Max Muller, the deputy Head of Outside Broadcasts, who took over as Head in 1952.

A Chinese wall soon developed between these two departments, and there was little or no co-operation and certainly no goodwill. The two disciplines of live commentaries and a considered expert report call for different qualities. Charles Max Muller became increasingly angry that Angus Mackay refused to use the Outside Broadcast commentator already in place, preferring to send his Fleet Street sports journalists. Angus could certainly pull in the best, and such well known names as Peter Wilson of the *Daily Mirror* (father of Julian Wilson of BBC Television) and J. L. Manning of the *Daily Mail* became regular contributors.

Still the row simmered on, with the BBC management failing to grasp the nettle and terse memos flowing from the Controller Sound (then Michael Standing), the Controller Programme

Planning (H. Rooney Pelletier), and the Head of Planning Light Programme (George Camacho). To say that Angus Mackay was a law unto himself was an understatement. He ploughed his own furrow, and the style of the original programme which he set and the standard that he demanded of his staff and contributors were the models for the successful, slick, punchy, disciplined reportage that has stood the test of time. Angus certainly had a nose for news and if you were lucky enough to provide him with a scoop he never failed to recognise it.

Though the origins of *Sports Report* lay in football, those early programmes covered a variety of different sports. The first racing 'piece' came in the evening programme on 6 March 1948. Billed in *Radio Times* as 'A Preview of the Flat Racing Season', it was delivered by John Hislop, a leading amateur rider and Racing Correspondent of the *Observer*. John later became a Member of the Jockey Club and the breeder of Brigadier Gerard. No doubt John Hislop referred to the Free Handicap and picked out the three leading contenders for the 1948 Classics, My Baby, The Cobbler and Black Tarquin. These three-year-olds all 'trained on'. In the colours of the Maharajah of Baroda My Babu beat The Cobbler by a head in the Two Thousand Guineas and Black Tarquin won the St Leger.

The 1948 flat racing season was the most successful ever staged with 2,203 races run. Prize money was almost £1.2 million and 4,400 horses competed. Racing was emerging from the war-time cutbacks with exceptional vigour. This surge in interest was not lost on Angus Mackay, who always tried to reflect the newspaper coverage in his programmes.

In October 1948 John Hislop was back to discuss the form for the Cambridgeshire Handicap. However looking ahead to a specific race – and one of the most important betting races at that – was like walking on very thin ice. At this time the BBC refused to acknowledge that betting on horse-racing actually happened, and in case the Corporation was accused of encouraging the public to gamble no hint or suggestion of anything as outrageous as a tip dare be given. I wonder John Hislop worked around that. Could he have indicated that the

three-year-old Sterope looked well handicapped? He was, and
carried 7 stone 4 to victory at 25/1. He was trained by Rufus
Beasley at Malton and returned to Newmarket the following
year, when he won again carrying 2 stone more.

In November 1948 Peter Dimmock, later Head of Outside
Broadcasts for BBC Television, contributed a piece in which he
discussed current form. The following month he and Peter
O'Sullevan, then Racing Correspondents for the Press
Association, both came on the programme billed in *Radio
Times* as: 'Racing: This week's news from courses and stables
by Peter O'Sullevan, presented by Peter Dimmock.'

In November 1949 Angus included extracts from the
afternoon's commentary by Peter Dimmock and Raymond
Glendenning on the Manchester November Handicap, and on
Boxing Day a clip of Raymond Glendenning's commentary on
the King George VI Chase from Kempton Park made the
programme. Racing was receiving a share of the limited time
available.

In 1950 four races were broadcast in the Home Service, a
new departure which presented a problem. The Head of Radio
Broadcasts agreed to end *Choral Evensong* at 3.40 p.m. in
order to take in the Ascot Stakes!

In 1955 a new landmark occurred. *Sports Report* was
extended from half an hour to an hour. Yet the controversy over
Mackay's use of Fleet Street journalists continued to occupy the
Controller of the Light Programme, who wrote that too many
newspaper correspondents were taking part in *Sports Report*.
Now he tried a different tack and asked about the fees paid to
these journalists. The answer came back from Angus that the
fees paid to his contributors averaged only £154 13 shillings
(£154.65) per programme.

On 22 August Charles Max Muller wrote to Angus Mackay
and asked 'why have you employed another person at Lord's
for the cricket when Peter West was there as a commentator?
Yet you sent Crawford White.'

Racing was still being broadcast on the Light Programme, but
by the mid-1950s Peter Dimmock and Peter O'Sullevan had
moved over to television, which was now covering some of the

principal races. For previews on the big handicaps Angus called on Tom Cosgrove, Racing Correspondent of the *Evening News*.

There was still a gap in the racing coverage. Though the racing results were given there was rarely a voice piece reporting on the big race of the day. Nor were there interviews with jockeys or trainers. There were good reasons for this. First, mobile tape-recording machines were not then available and it was often difficult to get someone either to the control room or to the commentary point. There was a huge reluctance, particularly by trainers, to be interviewed and perhaps unwittingly let slip a remark which might offend the owner of the horse or reveal future plans, so spoiling the starting price for a prospective gamble. Racing was far more secretive than now.

During my 40 years at the BBC I have served under nine Heads of Outside Broadcasts. It was Charles Max Muller who in 1969 (his last year in the job) created a new position, BBC Racing Correspondent, sharing the cost with Peter Dimmock at Television. I had been one of the panel of racecourse commentators for five years, and had worked as a paddock commentator for Independent Television and as the 'Third Man' in BBC Television's coverage of racing, giving the betting, providing interviews between races and standing in for either Peter O'Sullevan for the race or for Clive Graham in the paddock.

I was offered the job, which was mainly working for television with the opportunity of reporting on racing for radio. It was for one year as a trial. The problem was that Angus Mackay refused to use me, preferring his Fleet Street 'stringers'.

Eventually, so I have been told, Angus was summoned on high and told in no uncertain terms that as the BBC now had its first sports correspondent he was to use this new asset! In due course I went to see Angus, and the meeting hardly gave me much confidence. 'I think that racing is punk,' he told me, 'You have no journalistic experience. I have been told I have to use you, on no account will you overrun!'

In this inauspicious way I began the long haul. Within the year Raymond Glendenning had retired from giving horse-racing commentaries and the whole concept of my new post was changed overnight. I was offered the position of BBC Radio Racing

Correspondent, in charge of all radio racing commentaries as well as servicing the sports news and other news channels.

Television advertised for its own Racing Correspondent which went to my old colleague from racecourse commentary days, Peter Montague-Evans. Shortly afterwards Brian Moore became the BBC Football Correspondent, Brian Johnston started to cover cricket and Raymond Baxter motoring.

In 1969 Charles Max Muller retired and Robert Hudson became the new HOBS. He immediately began to plan to amalgamate the Outside Broadcast Department with Sports News. This was not put into effect until 1972 after Angus Mackay had retired. Cliff Morgan then became the new Editor of Sport with the capable Bob Burrows as his deputy. The racing schedule was transformed, more meetings were included and instead of simply broadcasting the main race of the day, supporting races were considered.

With the development of portable tape-recorders it was now possible to interview winning connections flushed with success in the winners' enclosure and the racing 'package', which included reports on the races linked to these interviews, now became a regular feature of *Sports Report*. We were helped by a totally different attitude to the media by the racing professionals. Trainers, jockeys and owners made themselves more readily available, and the content of these racing reports became far more informed and topical.

The names of those who have featured in *Sports Report* reads like a 'Who's Who' of racing. Lester Piggott rarely made it; Willie Carson always agreed to talk. His infectious, manic laugh became a regular radio sound, and his bubbling and engaging personality has now been transferred from his riding career to a new one in broadcasting with both BBC Television and Radio Five Live.

Interviewing jockeys is always difficult, since we broadcasters are not allowed into the weighing room. I particularly wished to interview the Australian jockey George Moore after he had won the King George and Queen Elizabeth Stakes on Busted in 1967. Highly strung, George had been sitting on his bench still in his silks until after the last race. The place was deserted when he emerged but it was worth the wait.

I was lucky after Nijinsky won the St Leger and the Triple Crown. I found his owner, Charles Engelhard, sitting in his Rolls drinking coke from a can, completely overcome with emotion. Choking back the tears he said, 'This is the most wonderful moment of my life.' I thought at the time that owning a great racehorse can seriously damage your health, and sadly soon afterwards this great supporter of English racing died.

When Robert Hudson retired in 1975, Cliff Morgan became Head of Radio Sport. Shortly after, when Cliff went to BBC Television, Bob Burrows took over. Under Bob Burrows the number of races that I broadcast increased from 50 a year when I joined in 1960 to 270. Like Angus Mackay before him, Bob had a tremendous feeling for a story. It was a serious blow to Radio Sport when he left suddenly to go to ITV in 1980.

The Grand National has always been a rich source of vivid and emotional interviews. Five o'clock on Grand National Saturday afternoon is essential listening for anyone who wishes to have the thrills and spills of The National distilled on radio. I shall never forget Tommy Stack's excited description of how he partnered Red Rum for the gelding's third Grand National. Mr Charlie Fenwick, the American amateur who rode Ben Nevis to win in 1980 from just four other finishers, recalled his trainer Tim Forster's instructions in the paddock before the race to 'keep remounting'. Another amateur, Mr Dick Saunders, spoke eloquently after Grittar's win in 1982, describing just what it meant to a hunting man to win the great race.

In 1981 it was the turn of Aldanti to tear at our heart strings, ridden as it was by Bob Champion, who had conquered cancer to return to race riding. This was a story which unfolded in *Sports Report*, with a fairy-tale ending that was made into the successful film *Champions*.

Jenny Pitman can always be relied on to give us our money's worth. She made memorable broadcasts after Corbiere won in 1983 and also after Royal Athlete galloped home in 1995. She also gave it to us with both barrels after her Esha Ness was first past the post in the void race of 1993. The Radio Five sports team at Aintree was given a Sony Award for our coverage of the aftermath of this notorious debacle.

The award for the most outrageous remark after winning The National surely goes to Mick Fitzgerald after he had partnered Rough Quest in 1996. He told us that the experience of the nine and a half minutes of riding Rough Quest over the Aintree fences was even better than sex!

There is one *Sports Report* that I will never forget. The date was Saturday 28 September 1996. I had broadcast the first three races from the Ascot Festival of Racing. The Italian-born jockey Frankie Dettori had won all of them in the dark blue colours of the Godolphin stable. We thought about asking for an interview for our 'package', but Frankie was rather busy, for he won the fourth and then the fifth race. The sixth race clashed with the reading of the football results, but when he won that too Joanne Watson, the producer of *Sports Report*, asked me to do a live commentary on the 5.35, the seventh race.

By now I had moved down from the commentary position to our tiny studio on the ground floor. I seized a racecard, glued it on to cardboard, and rushed back to the top of the stands. There were 18 runners and I did not know any of them. Working overtime I almost had them all committed to memory before the off.

As promised, Joanne Watson joined the commentary at half way and Frankie was in the lead on Fujiyama Crest, the top weight, and there he stayed. And so listeners to *Sports Report* were able to hear live a remarkable piece of racing history as Frankie, inspired by the occasion, drove Fujiyama Crest home to win all seven Ascot races – the 'Magnificent Seven' as it became known. Frankie kept everyone at Ascot that evening, and at eight o'clock I was still sending reports and interviews down the line on what was the most memorable raceday in my experience – and indeed of everyone present, as Clare Balding relates on pages 208–213.

Long may 'Out of the Blue' continue to be played on Saturday afternoons, the prelude to great sporting moments captured on radio from the heroes who provided the day's epic sporting memories.

Fifty years and counting.

JENNY PITMAN

A Date with Des

*Jenny Pitman is a leading National Hunt trainer who
has twice won the Grand National – with Corbiere
in 1983 and Royal Athlete in 1995. In addition, her
horse Esha Ness 'won' the void race in 1993.*

9 April 1983 was a memorable day for me. I became the first
woman to train the winner of the Grand National – something
I had always set my heart on. And I gave my first interview to
Desmond Lynam, who was presenting *Sports Report* that day.

I had been very confident about Corbiere's chances before
the race, but when he and Ben de Haan passed the post, just
holding off Greasepaint, I felt as though I was dreaming. I
remember being almost carried along by two big policemen –
people must have thought I'd been arrested – and eventually I
ended up in one of the BBC vans to appear on *Sports Report*.

Des greeted me with a kiss and a glass of champagne, and I
was able to hear Peter Bromley's commentary – which almost
persuaded me that it hadn't been a dream after all. Peter
presented me with his commentary chart as a permanent
memento: I had it framed and it now hangs in my study.

Best of all, a week later came the news that the Grand
National had been saved after months of uncertainty. Since that
day, I've met Des many times at Aintree: he's very genuine and
easy to talk to, and somehow our chats have become part of the
ritual. He says I always seem to have a front-row seat for the
National, and long may it continue!

MIKE INGHAM

Inside Out

*Mike Ingham, the BBC's urbane Football
Correspondent, spent four years presenting
Sports Report before taking to the road to cover
football full-time. Mike is a lawyer by training, a
DJ by inclination and a fashion icon.*

The school bus would deposit me at my stop, and after
grovelling around in the dust to reclaim the satchel, blazer and
cap inevitably thrown through the window by Derbyshire's
equivalent of the Bash Street Kids, I would set about the short
walk home – just enough time to introduce an imaginary *Sports
Report* under my breath. I would hand over to Geoffrey Green,
Charles Harold, Robin Marlar and Simon Smith – even take in
a final word from J. L. Manning, and nobody would run a
second over time. Angus Mackay would have been proud.
Every pretend *Sports Report*, Derby County, then a trundling
Second Division team, were always guaranteed the mock
headlines after another epic victory that kept them on course
for the European Cup, while Nottingham Forest were on the
end of a good hiding. Remember this was before *Match of the
Day*, so there was no danger of anyone with a beard popping
up on television later that night to shatter my illusions,
cocooned as I was in my crystal set world of Uncle Mac,
Educating Archie and, on Luxembourg, Horace Bachelor in
Keynsham – that's K-E-Y-N-S-H-A-M – Bristol.
   It might have been a wet Wednesday, but Saturday always

comes when you're a little boy walking home to his tea with stars in his eyes. Occasionally, just for variety, it would be *Sports Parade* looking ahead as opposed to looking back, whetting the appetite with our correspondents in Manchester, Birmingham and London, but more often than not it was the five o'clock show, and never a technical hitch. But why ten minutes up and over a hill visiting Arsenal, Ayresome and Anfield instead of declining *amo, amas, amat* – because, whereas *Civis Romanus* was about as stimulating as a local production by the Townswomen's Guild, radio was an empire of the senses. The only time television made such an adolescent impression on me was when I was not allowed to watch *Quatermass and the Pit*, listened from the bedroom through the floorboards, and imagined pictures far more hideous than were actually being transmitted.

Sound One – Vision Nil was a far more significant childhood result than overcoming the eleven-plus. Radio always killed the video star in my dreams, creating an art gallery of portraits, a library of drama and suspense. What's more, all you had to do was secretly lift up the desk lid at school during a physics lesson to plug into this land of make-believe – more illuminating than any bunsen burner. Simply compare and contrast an FA Cup draw on radio and TV – one is magical, the other is not. I rest my case. It was Fantasy Football thirty years ahead of its time – except that fantasy isn't supposed to become reality in the way that it did for me on Saturday, 19 July 1980.

Sports Report introduced by Mike Ingham – 'Out of the Blue'. It didn't matter that I had to wait another month for the football season to start. There I was in that electric chair on what was the opening day of the Moscow Olympics, and at home the 109th Open golf championship from Muirfield and cricket's Benson and Hedges Cup Final from Lord's – not bad for starters. Butterflies, adrenalin and pride – if I'd been run over by a bus on my walk home that night, well at least professional ambition had been fulfilled, never mind a certificate in education. This was graduation day in the academy of broadcasting. Wrong – this was merely the start of an apprenticeship. There may have been an extra spring in the

step on Monday morning, but the feet were about to be
returned very firmly to the ground.

Radio Sport was in a transition period awaiting a new head
of department, having just lost Bob Burrows to ITV. Cliff
Morgan was back in temporary charge and took me under his
wing. 'Right – time for you to start learning what broadcasting
is really all about,' was his morning greeting. 'Stand up against
the wall.' It was like a scene out of *The French Connection* with
Gene Hackman. But instead of being frisked, I was invited to
fill my lungs and breathe. 'It's a bit like being an opera singer,"
said Cliff, and he knew plenty of them. 'You can't perform if
you don't know how to breathe properly. And another thing –
it's PICTURE, not pitcher – pitcher is something you carry
water in.' All this in front of the rest of the sportsroom – or
rather classroom – within 48 hours of supposedly conquering
broadcasting's Everest. Humiliation – but while it felt that way
at the time, in retrospect it was a calculated yet caring reminder
of the privilege I should be feeling to be allowed to set foot in
the building let along preside over *Sports Report*.

I hope I learned my lesson and tried to avoid other well-
signposted pitfalls in those early days. A little knowledge can be
such a dangerous thing – don't overload a simple cue with
information – don't take the words out of your reporter's
mouth. I shuddered when I was told that one of my colleagues
once handed over to John Arlott for a cricket update at
Bournemouth along the lines of. 'Well now cricket and the last
time we were at Bournemouth, Hampshire having won the toss
and batted were having real problems on a drying wicket
against the Gloucestershire spin of David Allen – who
accounted for the early wickets of Marshall, Gray and
Horton... There was also an excellent catch by Graveney to
send back Harrison, but then Sainsbury and White started to
dig in and were able to resist with a half-century partnership –
anyway, over to the ground to get the position from John
Arlott.' The great man paused and with dignified disdain
remarked, 'You've said it all young man – back to you.'

By this time of course, after a decade of change in the 1970s,
Sports Report no longer stood in splendid isolation – it

climaxed four-and-a-half hours of *Sport on Two*. There was often talk of bringing in a fresh team after the football commentary ended, but it was decided for continuity to stick with the same presentation and production. There was a whole new audience though at five o'clock, timing their return journeys to car radios to coincide with the first reading of the football results, and for the host most certainly a new gear to move into: only too aware from my local radio days that numerous other stations will be joining for the first note of 'Out of the Blue' – absolutely vital that the band is not a second late in striking up and then into the headlines – don't shout – you are only talking to one person – then come in James Alexander Gordon, effortlessly gliding into tempo in harmony with the well-oiled machine that this institution of a broadcast has become.

Whatever mayhem may be occurring in the control room at this time, on the other side of the glass the link man, padded from it all by cotton wool, is steered reassuringly through rough water and calm by the producer. After a while, this relationship becomes almost telepathic, both parties being deeply aware of the footsteps they are following in, the standards and traditions that need to be upheld, the economy of words – principles laid down by the legendary and visionary Angus Mackay. I had the good fortune to meet him socially in his retirement – mellow, self-effacing and difficult to equate with the Dickensian schoolmaster figure that came across in all those immortal anecdotes related by more senior colleagues. I half expected him to say to me, 'If you don't eat your meat, you can't have any pudding'. Instead he gently observed that he still listened and yes, it was 'Just fine son' – a seal of approval worth more than a hundred BBC Programme Review boards.

We had, of course, refined some of his original ideas – no longer, for example, slavishly writing out in advance three different cues into football reports to cater for all eventualities. The multi-dimensional presenter had also become the teleprinter correspondent to speed up the results – we were even prepared to take live reports on the 'phone. Tony Adamson, I recall, was once halfway through his golf piece when his money ran out. But the essential elements remained unchanged. Down in studio B9 in the bowels of Portland Place, where you could at times still eerily hear the Bakerloo line, the ribbon microphone suspended Lord Reith-style in front of your lip made you feel guilty that you were not bow-tied for the occasion.

Sporting giants Bobby Moore, Danny Blanchflower, Floyd Patterson, Sir Leonard Hutton, Lew Hoad and Fred Perry were among those who braved a BBC cuppa at five o'clock with me in the studio. From the world of entertainment, Willie Rushton, Spike Milligan, Eric Morecambe and Georgie Fame made the airwaves snap, crackle and pop. Alan Price, I remember, even composed a special song which he played on the programme – 'Please Spare a Thought for the Losers'. (He was a Fulham fan, so it was an emotion he was becoming used to experiencing!) Naturally, the professional broadcasters lined up to have the final word – Ian Wooldridge, Patrick Collins, Frank Keating and Brian Johnston were treasured heavyweight contributors.

Dear old Johnners was even inspired to write a book after one of his visits when in the earlier part of the programme Ingers (as I was inevitably christened) linked him up with the outside world. *Chatterboxes – My Friends the Commentators*, published by Methuen, was the result in 1983. In the Introduction he wrote:

> On Saturday 27 December 1982 I was invited to be the studio guest in BBC Radio 2's *Sport on Two*. During the afternoon, the presenter Mike Ingham suggested that I might like to try out his job and cue over to the commentator at the various sporting events around the country. I did not do it very well, but I thoroughly enjoyed myself because I found that I knew them all personally. After the programme, it dawned on me that I not only just knew but had probably worked with all the television and radio commentators who had broadcast from the time when I joined the BBC in 1946 – so I thought it would be fun, at least for me, to look back on my 37 colleagues, not forgetting the slight mishaps or gaffes

which have occurred. But there will be no sensational
revelations. This book will be just an appreciation – in
both senses of the word – of my friends the commentators.

And how they appreciated him. Brian achieved instant rapport
in that show with every voice fed into headphones – he knew
them all, and the respect was mutual, underlining the priceless
advantage of winning your stripes and being known in the field.
It's never easy to interview somebody down the line when your
guest is struggling to put a face to your voice. You get the job
done, but there's a missing ingredient. Perhaps that was why it
was time in 1984 to leave the bunker and go out on the road.
After all, historically the *Sports Report* presenter had been a
veteran of World Cups and Olympic Games: my career was
back to front – expediently, with hindsight.

There were limited opportunities to get out and about with
the programme. However, *Sport on Two* and *Sports Report*
were always introduced live from the Grand National at
Aintree, and though I'll never forget John Timpson back-
announcing me after I'd given the racing tips on the *Today*
programme on Radio Four as 'Mike Ingham for a horse...', I
knew as much about racing as I do about Albanian history. Still,
two days before my Grand National debut, Peter Bromley
introduced me to an owner, Mr Richard Shaw, in our team hotel
– Hello Dandy was his horse. We had a little chat, and the next
time we met, both of us choking back the tears, was in the
winning enclosure 48 hours later.

Another memory from around that time was when I was
entrusted with the velvet bag, box and balls overnight before
the draw for the third round of the FA Cup was made live in our
studio. I was so excited, I remember taking them with me to the
Radio 1 studio where I was making a brief appearance on Andy
Peebles' Friday night show to look ahead to the weekend.
Showing off, we opened the box on the air – great radio, I'm
sure you'll agree – and one ball fell out and on to the floor.
Fortunately, we found it before the cleaner did, otherwise
Tottenham wouldn't have been in the Cup that season.

When I was a child my favourite *Sports Report* personality

was Bill Bothwell, the football reporter in the north-west who
was also a director of Tranmere Rovers. Listening to his
reports, you could almost smell the half-time Bovril in the
stadium. It was a delight to meet this charming man who, in the
final season before he sadly died, volunteered in the middle of
winter to travel from the Wirral to East Anglia, as he'd never
covered a game at Ipswich Town. He arrived just in time to hear
that the match had been called off, rang in, and with not a hint
of frustration in his voice asked whether there was anywhere
else the producer would like him to drive to. They don't make
him like that any more.

My favourite guest – and there is no contest – was
Muhammad Ali, who came in ostensibly to promote a film and
began by mumbling without any conviction or interest a few
well-rehearsed public relations answers to my rather
predictable questions. The interview was on the ropes, until we
changed tracks and I had the temerity to suggest that many
people thought he was ill-advised to be getting into the ring
again with Larry Holmes. He shuffled into his stride and
filibustered memorably the way only he could. The great
tragedy is that his subsequent story and life might have been so
different if he had resisted that challenge, but it was his drug
and he wanted one last fix.

Ali let me get away with lazily falling back on the 'many
people' cliche when asking that question. Brian Clough would
never have let that pass. 'Who are these people – name them,'
he would probably have said. Interviewing Cloughie live in
Sports Report in his prime was just about the most
intimidating, yet at the same time rewarding, mission you could
undertake. Nine times out of ten he would almost certainly turn
you down with a smile and add, 'But thank you for asking
young man' – but you would always go back with that tenth
request knowing that, if he agreed, provided you were on your
toes, the result could be pure gold dust. One of my favourite
Clough stories goes back to his Derby days when journalist
Michael Carey was ghosting a local weekly column for him.
They would get together briefly to compare notes, and on one
occasion Brian enthusiastically greeted the writer with 'Hey

Michael, I've got your intro for you already ... it goes like this ... what a week it's been for saying bugger me...'

After vacating the best seat in Broadcasting House, my first Saturday afternoon commentary on 25 August 1984 found me watching Manchester United against Watford from the best seat at Old Trafford – at least it was in those days, but that's another story! Gordon Strachan, United's new signing, was centre stage in my first goal clip, so sparing me the potential nightmare of mistaken identity. How can you mess up a penalty taken by a household name with ginger hair? My first season ended horrifically alongside Peter Jones in Belgium at the Heysel disaster. I still think of Peter the master craftsman almost every time I pick up the microphone at a big game – had he not died so prematurely, how he would have loved to have commentated on Cantona and Zola in English football, and what fun he would have had with Gazza and Ian Wright. I'm not sure what he would have made of having to arrive at Anfield for a Liverpool v Manchester United game on a Saturday morning by 9 o'clock for an 11.15am kick off – anti-social in the extreme, but a good example of the changing times.

Another Peter – Lorenzo – who'd forgotten more about football journalism that I could ever hope to learn, was with me during those early commentaries. Charismatic Peter, who hardly ever saw a bad game, especially at his cherished West Ham, often began his reports with 'Call me Lucky Lorenzo' – so we did, and it stuck to this day. The two Peters are greatly missed. I remember the elegant Mr Lorenzo lovably stuck in a 1966 time warp on a rainy day in the office, with a captive audience and little to occupy his editorial mind, trying to remember the eleven Argentinians who became ten at Wembley after Rattin was sent off. One final name eluded him, and he refused to look it up. 'I know,' he said, 'pass me the 'phone'. Out came the best contacts book in the business, *brring, brring*, 'Hello Alf, how are you – listen, who was that Argentinian number 9...'

The industry does allow you to stand toe to toe with your idols. At European Championships and World Cups there are always press tournaments accompanying the main event – and

with so many former star players now *bona fide* members of the
media, it can be theme for a dream time. In Sweden in 1992, for
example, when the English journalists took on the French, the
great Giresse and Tigana were members of the opposition. Sir
Bobby Charlton took his place in the English side, but this cut
no ice with one of Fleet Street's finest, who at one point
screamed across the pitch to one of the footballers of the
twentieth century, 'Hey Charlton, give me the ball at my feet.'

When people say there aren't the same idiosyncratic
characters in the game these days, I have to agree. There
certainly aren't the managers around like Tommy Docherty or
club directors like the gregarious John and Patrick Cobbold at
Ipswich Town. They would never have tolerated BBC Radio
Sport being shortchanged and downgraded in the pecking
order of media priorities, especially when the time was fast
approaching 5 o'clock and that signature tune – like Bryon
Butler's voice, as comforting as a warm overcoat in winter.
Where once upon a time football personalities would clamber
over seats to get to our outside broadcast in time to be
interviewed, nowadays in the more competitive, corporate,
commercial world we are often reduced to being one of a pool
of microphones in car parks or corridors, clutching at straws
for a soundbite.

'Radio the medium that is now *large*,' I heard someone
proclaim recently – a good marketing slogan, and I would love
to think that was still football's perception of us. I do worry
greatly that future generations may not inherit radiowaves in
their bloodstream – that young people won't have been
encouraged at home in the way we were to *listen* as well as
watch with Mother. My greatest professional wish for the next
century would be for *Sports Report* to reach its century as well.

TREVOR BAILEY

Sir Gary Sobers

A genuine all-rounder for Essex and England and also a talented footballer, Trevor Bailey was a dogged batsman and a reliable fast medium bowler with best Test figures of 7–34. Trevor is a long-serving contributor to Test Match Special, *where he rejoices in his mysterious nickname of 'The Boil'.*

Throughout the 1960s Sir Gary Sobers bestrode the international cricket scene like a colossus, which was hardly surprising, as in the entire history of the game there has never been a finer, more complete or more exciting all-rounder. And, I believe, there never will be. In his reign of just over 20 years he enchanted the world, not only with the innings he produced, the wickets he captured, and the catches he held, but also with the grace and the elegance with which these were obtained. He created more moments of pure magic than any other cricketer since the war and would be an automatic choice, along with Sir Donald Bradman, Sir Jack Hobbs, and Sydney Barnes, for the finest World XI of all time.

Gary was first selected for the West Indies at the age of 17 as an orthodox slow left-arm bowler and batted at number 9, an event I remember very clearly, because England won the match to square the series, I returned my best figures in the Caribbean, and I was Gary's first victim. However, within a few years he had blossomed forth to become not only the best and most attractive left-hand batsman of his era, but also one of the best of all time. At 21 he made 365 against Pakistan, which until it was beaten by Brian Lara in 1994, was the highest score in Test cricket. During his long international career he averaged over 57. I have no doubt that this would have been higher, and he would have made even more runs, if he had batted higher in the order on more occasions, instead of going in at number 6. He did this as captain, because it enabled him to rally and inspire the bowlers in his team, which he did on numerous occasions; he was also a very unselfish player.

Although he batted like a cavalier, behind the gaiety was a steady purposefulness, which I discovered for the first time when I was bowling against him on a helpful pitch in the Lord's Test and he made a technically superb 61 in just under four hours. His determination when batting was very much in evidence at another Lord's Test. On that occasion he nursed the comparatively inexperienced David Holford into a record-breaking partnership of 275. My favourite example of his fighting qualities, both as player and as captain, occurred in the 2nd Test at Sabina Park in 1968. He arrived at the crease on a king pair, his team had been made to follow on by England and were facing almost certain defeat. His reply was to conjure up an undefeated 113 before making a brave declaration with 9 wickets down, and then he removed both Boycott and Cowdrey for 0 in his first over, after opening the bowling, and almost won the match.

Gary was very difficult to bowl against, because he had the ability to hit a good ball to the boundary along the ground off either his front or back foot, and using the full face of his bat. He had a high backlift with a full follow through, which is one of the reasons why he became the first man to hit six sixes in one over, while playing for Notts. against Glamorgan at Swansea, certainly not one of the smallest grounds.

Although Gary's bowling was not as spectacular as his batting, it was even more remarkable and he was unquestionably the most complete bowler I have ever seen – he was good enough to justify selection for the West Indies purely as a bowler in three entirely different styles. He began as an orthodox slow left-arm spinner for Barbados and the West Indies, probably because there were plenty of seamers around at that time who could also bat, including Sir Frank Worrell, Gerry Gomez and Denis Atkinson. It is impossible to estimate how good he might have become, if he had concentrated on that method, but his figures in his first Test of 28.5–9–75–4 against an England total of 414 were quite impressive.

Having established himself as the leading batsman in the world, and as his captain, Frank Worrell, wanted to do less bowling Gary began to develop from a useful support seamer into the best left-arm paceman in the world, once Alan Davidson had retired. He had a sensibly economic run up, a classical, flowing action, a graceful follow through, and the ability to swing the occasional ball back into the right-hander from on, and just outside his off stump. His pace was not far short of that provided by Wes Hall and Charlie Griffith, and when he really decided to stretch himself, probably as quick. As if that was not enough, Gary began experimenting with wristspin; the fact that Adelaide is not exactly a happy hunting ground for seam may have had something to do with it. The outcome was that for about five years, until his shoulder started to give him serious trouble, he was among the finest wristspinners in the world. He also became the first all-rounder to complete the Australian 'double' of over 1,000 runs and 50 wickets, which is infinitely more demanding than the English version.

Gary moved so well, and so easily when batting and bowling, that it is inevitable he was also a quite exceptional all-purpose fieldsman with a lovely pair of hands and lightning reflexes. He averaged more than one catch per Test, many of these at backward short leg to Lance Gibbs. Gary was involved in so many record breaking partnerships, such as his stand of 399 with Frank Worrell against England in Barbados, that it is hard to select the finest, but I cannot imagine anybody batting better than he did when he scored 254 at Melbourne against the Rest of the World. Sir Donald Bradman reckoned that to have been just about the finest innings he had ever seen, and he should certainly know.

TONY ADAMSON

The Ryder Cup

*Tony Adamson, the BBC's Golf Correspondent,
has also commentated on tennis, football and
rowing and is a former* Sports Report *presenter.
He is a devotee of country music and one of the
very few 18-handicappers to have birdied the
fearsome 18th hole on the West course at
Wentworth.*

The Ryder Cup has reduced strong men to tears and rendered
radio reporters speechless. In 1991 on the Ocean course at
Kiawah Island, South Carolina, the final match was on the final
green and Bernhard Langer was faced with a 5 foot putt. If he
holed it Europe retained the trophy. If he missed America
regained it.

The tension was unbearable. Players dared not look. Wives
of players buried their heads in their husbands' shoulders.
Hardened pressmen could hardly believe it had come to this,
and radio commentators lost the power of speech. High up in
my eyrie behind the eighteenth green, I was aware of a sudden
drying of the throat, churning of the stomach and a lack of
liaison between the brain and the voicebox. Only the sound of
nervous heavy breathing and the pounding of the Atlantic surf
assured the listener the radio was switched on. Desperately
seeking help, I glanced at co-commentator Tommy Horton,
only to discover the veteran Ryder Cup player trembling
slightly, open mouthed and lost for words. Eventually, with the

help of an alarm call from the producer, the brain re-engaged and the mouth responded. 'If anyone can hole this putt,' I said, abandoning all trace of impartiality, 'then surely it's Bernhard Langer.' The German had forced his way back from two down with four to play to all square playing the last. Langer and caddie Pete Coleman inspected the line as if it were a minefield. 'It looks like five feet, could be a little longer,' I said trying to keep the microphone still in a shaking hand. 'He's over it now.' Langer settled on the putt grasping the putter with that distinctive style designed to defy the dreaded yips, right hand clutching left forearm. Seconds later Langer looked to the heavens and let out a howl of anguish. So did the commentator. 'He's missed on the right!' I screamed. 'He's missed on the right,' as pandemonium broke out. For the first time since 1983 America held the Ryder Cup. They had won what had been absurdly labelled 'the war on the shore' by an American newspaper, and America's captain Dave Stockton and his players waded into the Atlantic, trophy and all to celebrate. Meanwhile, as Langer remained rooted to the spot in abject despair Severiano Ballesteros was one of the first to console him and lead him to Europe's team headquarters. 'He put his arm around my shoulder,' said Langer, 'and then he started to cry. As soon as he did so did I, maybe if he hadn't started I wouldn't have, I don't know.' Langer was then persuaded to join some of the team in a huge public marquee where the American supporters were celebrating and the Europeans were drowning their sorrows. Both sets of fans gave Langer a riotous welcome, not just out of sympathy for what he had suffered – according to Ballesteros the putt was impossible and no player could have holed it in that situation – but because Langer is one of the game's leading ambassadors. He climbed onto a table to acknowledge the ovation, the table collapsed and Langer slid to the floor. It had not been his day.

Not only had it been perhaps the most dramatic finish to any Ryder Cup, it was staged at one of the most unusual venues, a new purpose built Pete Dye course, lush fairways rising out of a wilderness blending sandy wastelands, instead of rough, encroaching marsh and water hazards some of which provided homes for local alligators. 'It's not like something in Ireland or Scotland,' said David Feherty, 'it's like something from Mars'.

For the first time in America, BBC Radio provided commentary from the course, filing 22 hours of live coverage during the three days. Producing a continuous seven-hour speech-based sports show was totally unknown in the States; their host broadcaster NBC looked upon it with some doubt and suspicion. Having requested them to provide a scaffold and a broadcasting box behind the eighteenth green from where I was due to anchor the programme we discovered on arrival a rickety, lopsided, tubular steel contraption and a ladder that looked as unstable as the remainder of the structure. The platform was bare and there was no sign of a commentary box.

Panic? Not a bit of it. Our intrepid BBC engineers, the best in the world, were as resourceful as ever. With the ingenuity of a Lawrence of Arabia, a roll of masking tape, umpteen layers of old strips of tarpaulin and cardboard and carpet, they created a kind of Bedouin tent on stilts, the opening of which gave one a clear view of the undulating slopes and dunes of the eighteenth fairway with the slate grey waters of the Atlantic in the distance.

Unfortunately the wind blew at Kiawah Island, and from all quarters. On one occasion, mid-programme, a gale force gust ripped large portions of tarpaulin from my tent and sent them winging their way like confetti towards the Atlantic, followed by pages of painstaking research. Not even the valiant efforts of an engineer, dashing down the eighteenth fairway with the determination of a Linford Christie, hurling himself left and right and into the air like a demented goalkeeper in rehearsal, could retrieve them.

But our fifteen-man team were pioneers, prepared to go where no radio golf team had ever gone before. Not even losing his voice could force George Bayley, the doyen of golf commentators, off the fairway for very long. Only one team member failed to stay the course. He was a young local student, one of a number who volunteered to carry the commentators' backpacks. Shortly after completing the marathon half mile walk between the ninth green and the tenth tee he answered a call of nature and that was the last his commentator Julian Tutt saw of him.

Bernard Gallacher, captain that year for the first time, will have mixed views on what has been known as good 'ole Southern hospitality. Gallacher was invited only once to play Kiawah Island prior to the match and that was six months before the tournament. Four days before the event, having arrived in luxury on Concorde, his team discovered their headquarters were so small, according to David Feherty they had to go outside to change their minds. In addition, one local radio disc jockey invented a 'wake up the enemy' campaign. Michael D of 95 SX would call the players' hotel at 6.00am in an attempt to disrupt their night's sleep, harass them, and 'give the Americans an early advantage' as he put it. He somehow gained access to the rooms where Seve Ballesteros, Ian Woosnam and Nick Faldo were sleeping but in each case only succeeded in talking to their wives. Shortly afterwards the DJ was on the receiving end of a dawn call from a British radio station and the score was settled all square.

The rancour spilled over into the matches. Even Dave Stockton adopted a jingoistic attitude, supporting the wearing of military style caps by some members of his team. Chants of war on the shore were heard as European players walked onto the greens and there was an altercation between Ballesteros and Jose Maria Olazabal and their American opponents, Paul Azinger and Chip Beck over the decision to change the American ball.

Two years later at the Belfry the two captains, Gallacher and Tom Watson, restored dignity to the match which the United States won by two points. Watson, winner of eight major championships, said 'this is the finest experience I have had in a game of golf'. The three days of competition yielded memories galore, especially the last afternoon which one recognised golf writer described as 'as good as it gets'. With Sam Torrance having to withdraw from the singles because of a toe injury, Lanny Wadkins, understanding his captain's dilemma, volunteered to step down from the American side in place of one of the younger members of the team. His generous gesture brought tears to his captain's eyes. Eight of the eleven singles went to the eighteenth and Tommy Horton and I shared with the players moments of sheer joy and deep despair. We watched Ian Woosnam hole a knee trembling putt for a half with Fred Couples which the American prayed Woosnam would miss. Our hearts bled for Barry Lane who squandered a lead of three up with five to play and lost to Chip Beck at the eighteenth, and for Costantino Rocca, one up with two to play who lost to Davis Love III at the last. Europe might well have won the Cup had not Lane and Rocca flinched with the winning post in sight. Such is the agony of the Ryder Cup when players play, not for themselves but for their country, their continent their team and their tour, and for no financial reward, when millions of television viewers in 120 countries sit, fascinated by the sight of great athletes, relentlessly competitive, scrupulously fair, stretched to the limit of their physical and mental endurance.

Radio 5 Live's recent series, *The Ryder Cup Years,* told the story of how the competition was born. It resulted from a chance remark made to Samuel Ryder, a wealthy seed merchant in St Albans, by his trinity church minister the Reverend Frank Wheeler. Ryder, who was fifty at the time, had suffered a breakdown in health, and Wheeler suggested he needed fresh air and exercise. 'Come and hit a few golf balls with me,' he said. Ryder's health immediately improved and he became so passionate about the game that he was appointed captain of Verulam Golf Club and sponsored tournaments to enhance the pay and status of the professional. Verulam became a popular haunt of the Great Triumvirate, J H Taylor, Harry Vardon and James Braid. Ryder even employed his own professional, Abe Mitchell, at the handsome annual salary of £500. By 1926 Ryder had become an influential figure in British professional golf. He hosted a champagne party at Wentworth that year following an informal match between American players, in Britain for the Open, and a British team which won by thirteen matches to one. America's captain Walter Hagan agreed and Samuel Ryder offered to donate a gold trophy. The Ryder Cup was born, a competition based on the cut and thrust of matchplay when a gesture or a comment or a mere shake of the head can have as much bearing on the result as holing a long putt, a sporting occasion that was to capture the public's imagination and leave them with indelible memories of great players and daring deeds.

There was Walter Hagan who captained the American team in the first six matches from 1927, resplendent in his gold cufflinks, silk shirts, flannelled trousers and two-tone shoes. On tour he needed a separate limousine just to transport his golfing wardrobe. He personally selected the team and used to shout 'who's going to be second' before he teed off. Among his four winning teams was Gene Sarazan the first man to win all four majors, Sam Snead of whom Ben Crenshaw once wrote 'he played golf the way you dream about playing it just once in your life,' and Byron Nelson who once won eleven tournaments in a row.

Ben Hogan led the Americans three times after the war, the last in 1967, the year Arnold Palmer questioned his decision to use the smaller British ball to which Hogan replied, 'Who said you're playing, Palmer?' Hogan spoke little on or off the course, rarely signed an autograph and practised golf until his hands bled.

Britain was dazzled by an array of great American players who dominated the match after the War, but they had their moments. At Lindrick in 1957 Britain recorded their first post-War victory after seven consecutive defeats by which time, as Peter Dobreiner wrote 'the American sporting public had begun to regard the Ryder Cup as an inconsequential act between consenting adults to be conducted in private. The British public saw it as the Third World War.' So confident were the United States of victory in 1957 they renewed the insurance policy on the trophy before they left home. But Britain's captain, Dai Rees, a feisty Welshman had other ideas. He even banned all wives from the players' hotel in an effort to generate team spirit. Britain lost the opening foursomes three-one and Desmond Hackett of the *Express* wrote that if Europe were to win he'd eat his brown derby. They duly took the match seven and a half, four and a half and

The Times correspondent wrote 'frankly you could have knocked us all down with a feather.'

Britain were not to win again until 1985 at the Belfry, by which time the contest had become a more significant, competitive affair with the introduction of the leading European players. Seve Ballesteros had emerged as the world's finest exponent of matchplay and the most feared Ryder Cup opponent. Two years previously in Florida the United States had scraped a victory but now, Europe, under Tony Jacklin's inspired leadership, triumphed emphatically by five points and not for twenty years had there been such excitement and scenes at a Ryder Cup. Sam Torrance, pencil lodged behind the ear, came from three down with eight to play to hole the winning putt across the eighteenth green to beat the US Open Champion Andy North. It was the Scotsman's finest hour and as he raised two arms to the sky in triumph, tears streaming down his face, he was engulfed by exultant team mates. In the BBC Radio commentary box Renton Laidlaw, another Scot, excitedly described the bedlam in front of him but when he turned for a comment from his co-commentator, John Fenton, the veteran broadcaster was emotionally spent, words refused to come and the lump in his throat grew even larger when Concorde flew over, dipping its silver wings in moving salute as it did so.

Even better was to follow two years later when Europe retained the trophy by winning on American soil for the first time in the history of the event. Ireland's Eamonn Darcy holed the decisive putt at the eighteenth and admitted afterwards not realising his opponent Ben Crenshaw had played the last twelve holes without his putter, which he had shattered in temper on the sixth. A sobbing Tony Jacklin, the skipper, could only mutter again and again 'This is the greatest day in my life,' as he savoured the fifteen-thirteen victory while his opposite number Jack Nicklaus suffered the indignity of losing on the course he designed and built at Muirfield Village. Indeed so quiet had the US support been on the first day following which their team trailed six-two, that Nicklaus ordered a consignment of miniature Stars and Stripes flags to be distributed among them to generate some passion, but the damage had already been done.

Jacklin's fourth and final year in charge was 1989 when Europe retained the Cup after a tied match at the Belfry. This time it was Christy O'Connor's turn to spill tears after a dazzling two iron to within a few feet of the flag at the eighteenth crushed the confident Fred Couples and gained Europe the half they were seeking.

Then it was to Kiawah Island and the Belfry again in 1993 for two American victories, since when Europe have ruled the roost as underdogs. At Oak Hill the Cup was regained by a team of golfers widely written off as poorly chosen and badly led. Needing to win seven and a half of the twelve singles they achieved exactly that to win by a point.

I have never felt such an atmosphere at a Ryder Cup in the United States. Huge, fair animated crowds massed round every green. In the crucial match Philip Walton aged years as his three hole lead with three to play over Jay Haas became two with two to play then one with one to play. He had a four foot putt at the seventeenth to win the Cup for Europe. Commentator George Bayley could hardly watch. 'I can't stand this,' he whispered as Walton prepared to putt. 'We need this point,' he said. 'That is Europe need this point. I've been told not to say we.' Nobody minded, Walton missed. And so the eighteenth. Walton had two putts for a half and a European victory and as his second from six inches was conceded he disappeared under a pile of bodies and the whooping and hollering began. 5 Live's microphones captured the moment as Bernard Gallacher, third time lucky as captain, could hardly speak for joy. 'We won it – we won it – we just won it'. Severiano Ballesteros chipped in 'Iz funtustic, iz grite, iz onbellavabul'. Nick Faldo, unashamedly tearful, was asked about his ninety yard pitch to the eighteenth against Curtis Strange. 'The finest shot I've ever played,' he said. And what of the following four foot putt that won the vital point? 'Everything moved but the putter,' he replied. 'My legs were shaking so much I thought they were somebody else's'.

'I watched the Ryder Cup on Radio 5 Live' wrote Kate Battersby of the *Daily Telegraph* the following day, drawing attention to the absence of terrestrial television's coverage of the event. 'Driving along London's Marylebone Road I noticed several drivers around me leaning forward, their faces frozen, and as Faldo's putt dropped there was much clenching of fists and banging of steering wheels. Then as we all realised that we were among many listening to the same station, we all laughed at each other.' '...the Radio 5 commentary team was magnificent' wrote Peter Barnard of *The Times*, 'I cannot think that a single sports event has ever been conveyed so well on the radio'. The response from listeners was also overwhelming and the coverage won Sony Awards for Best Sports Programme and Best Coverage of a Live Event in 1996.

The same radio team assembled at Valderrama on Spain's Costa del Sol in September 1997 for the Severiano Ballesteros show. Since being appointed captain the glamorous Spaniard had wrestled not always successfully with the burden of responsibility. Squabbles broke out intermittently and he seemed uncomfortable in the role. However, as battle commenced Seve dominated the match, charging round the course on his buggy, appearing to be in three places at the same time, yet the matches maintained a dignity and an etiquette second to none. Tom Kite was a model American captain acknowledging in defeat the superior golf by Europeans on the first two days. Europe led by five points going into the singles but it was left to Europe's number one Colin Montgomerie in the tenth singles to clinch a one point victory by gaining a half with Scott Hoch. The rain in Spain had dampened an otherwise dramatic and exciting spectacle and Seve declared the captain's chair vacant for the match at Brookline, Massachusetts, in two years' time.

So, seventy years on, the Ryder Cup which began as the casual though fiercely competitive series of games between fellow professionals has gathered momentum over the decades and is now as fervently supported by players and spectators alike as the game itself was revered by Samuel Ryder. In 1931, in his only radio interview, Ryder said of his gift of a trophy to launch the matches 'I have done several things in my life for the benefit of my fellow men but I am certain I have never done a happier thing than this.' Here, here.

IAN ROBERTSON

Evolution into Revolution

Ian Robertson's elusive qualities were first seen to advantage when he represented Scotland at fly half, before turning to journalism and broadcasting. He is an enthusiastic golfer and racegoer and sometime owner of various slow-moving racehorses.

Evolution is a concept I am able to handle and come to terms with because the change is gradual and is an integral part of a logical progression. Revolution, on the other hand, is very much more dramatic, less savoury and often defies logic.

It is against this background that rugby union has to be examined, for the whole rugby world has been totally and irrevocably transformed in the past two years. The game as it was in the good old days of Prince Obolensky and indeed of William Webb Ellis has been turned inside out and upside down and what is left after a revolution of outrageous ferocity is barely recognisable from the halcyon days of half a century ago, when *Sports Report* carried its first rugby contribution.

In 1995 the game switched from being amateur to professional. One day everyone played for fun and received no financial reward, and the next day the game was professional and those same players were being offered unlimited pots of gold at the end of seemingly endless rainbows.

The top international players earned zilch from playing rugby in the 1994–95 season. In the season just finished

(1996–97) those same players are each earning between £100,000 and £250,000 a year. It's a funny old world.

The hope is that rugby will retain much of its great tradition and heritage and that the moral code and ethos that has brought it successfully through so many years will not change simply because players are now being paid to play. Sadly, the laws of mutability are not that encouraging.

It is common knowledge that nothing is forever, but it strikes me that no other sport in the 1990s has changed quite so dramatically as rugby union. Indeed one of the great voices on rugby on *Sports Report* in 1948 bears ample testimony to that. I am thinking of Jock Wemyss and wondering what he would have made of Tuigamala joining Newcastle in 1997 at a cost estimated to be the best part of £2 million.

Jock was one of the great characters of the game and an outstanding Scottish international forward both before and after the First World War. He won his first two caps against Wales and Ireland in February 1914, but then, like every other able-bodied young man, he spent the next four years fighting for King and Country in the Great War. He did so at considerable personal cost. He lost an eye and one leg was liberally sprinkled with shrapnel. After convalescence and physiotherapy, he eventually became fit enough and strong enough to resume his rugby career.

So well did he recover he was selected to play against France in 1920 in Paris. I should point out that in those days (and also, I hasten to add, during my own three seasons in the Scotland side in the late 1960s), when each player was first selected he was given a pair of navy-blue stockings to last his whole international career and a Scottish jersey to last that particular season.

Jock arrived in the changing-room in Paris, and half an hour before the kick-off he asked the secretary of the Scottish Rugby Union for a pair of navy-blue stockings to go with the jersey he had just been handed. The aforesaid secretary, by all accounts, positively heaved with laughter and, catching his breath, replied, 'I wasn't born yesterday, you know. You'll wear the pair of stockings you wore in your last game for Scotland just like everyone else. Don't try to be a smart arse with me.' The fact that since Jock's previous game for Scotland six years had elapsed, World War I had been fought and won, and Jock had left several pints of blood, part of a leg and the whole of an eye on the battlefields of Europe seemed to count for little. Those were the true Corinthian days of the real amateur rugby player. That particular story almost had a happy ending. On returning shortly before the kick-off the official spotted Wemyss ready to take the field in shorts, jersey, boots but no stockings, just bare legs. He handed over a pair of stockings. However when, back in Scotland, Jock went to collect his travelling expenses, the secretary handed over his full claim less the cost of one pair of navy-blue stockings.

In those far off days of 1948, the international teams met at lunchtime on a Friday. All the players were introduced to each other, they ran twice round the pitch and then headed to the bar to discuss their tactics over a few pints. In my time, in the late 1960s, for all rugby players a coach was something that transported you from the hotel to the stadium. Not any more. Nowadays the coach is the key individual who decides on the team's whole approach to the match. But he is just one of an army of backroom boys. There are physiotherapists, sports psychologists, medics and even nutritionists. In Willie-John McBride's day the definition of a balanced diet was a pint of Guinness in each hand. A good definition and, come to think of it, a good diet.

But that was rugby the day before yesterday. Tomorrow is a very different story. Overnight rugby has become a multi-million-pound business. Not surprisingly, professional rugby has mirrored and aped so many other professional team sports. Just like soccer and rugby league in Britain or baseball or American football in the States, it is a very big business which depends on big money for survival. Wealthy individuals have become involved in England, attracted by the glamour and excitement of running a club and participating in a high-profile sport. Much of this has been for the good of the game and it is a positive bonus to find a genuine rugby enthusiast such as Nigel Wray, the wealthy chairman of the Burford Group, sinking his own money into Saracens rugby club to give them a real chance of becoming one of the top half dozen clubs in England. Nigel Wray is a fanatic who has played and followed the game for thirty years, and unquestionably he has the good of the game at heart.

On the other hand, one wonders if some of the other millionaire owners share this enlightened philosophy. One or two seem to have no rugby background, and little understanding of the right direction for the game to take. These people can be a positive threat and danger to the well-being and future development of the game.

None the less, the biggest single problem facing the game at club level is lack of money. It has been estimated that at the end of the first year of professional rugby the top 24 clubs in England have a combined deficit of over £15 million. This is not surprising when one considers that the average wage bill for a First Division club is about £1.5 million a year, and about half that for a Second Division side. Two years ago there was no wage bill for players at all.

The short-term saviour has been money from television, but the fact that there has been precious little interest from the terrestrial channels to buy secondary rights to English club rugby should have the alarm bells ringing very loudly indeed for the top clubs. There is no great interest in domestic club rugby when it is shown live , so it is easy to understand why virtually no-one is the slightest bit interested in recorded highlights. International rugby is big business but the domestic club game is not.

Against this background it is perhaps possible to understand the mounting problems confronting the modern director of rugby of a First Division club. It is also easy to put it into context if a Mr Micawber approach and attitude is adopted. For these modern post-Micawber economists, let me briefly recap the basic tenets of the Dickensian balance sheet: 'Annual income, twenty pounds, annual expenditure, nineteen pounds nineteen and six, result happiness. Annual income twenty pounds, annual expenditure twenty pounds and six pence, result misery.'

So it is in the Allied Dunbar Premiership. Income from

*Don Bradman, captain of the all-conquering Australians
in the summer of 1948.*

Emil Zatopek digging deep for victory in the Olympic 10,000 metres at Wembley Stadium, 1948.

Denis Compton of Middlesex, Arsenal and England in Brylcream pose.

Randolph Turpin in training for his successful world middleweight bout against Sugar Ray Robinson in 1951.

Duncan Edwards, 'Busby Babe' and England's youngest international footballer this century: a supreme talent, sadly unfulfilled.

The original housewife superstar: Fanny Blankers-Koen (nearest camera), winner of four gold medals at the 1948 Olympic Games.

Muhammad Ali sends Joe Bugner reeling during their World Heavyweight title fight in Kuala Lumpur, 1975.

Garfield Sobers with the Wisden Trophy after leading West Indies to a 3–1 series victory over England in 1966.

The best seat in the house. Renton Laidlaw broadcasts from his cardboard 'studio' at the US Open.

Jim Laker, BBC Sports Personality of the Year in 1956 after his 19 wickets against Australia at Old Trafford.

Elegant and refined, but plenty of steel. Peter May, captain of Surrey and England.

Nijinsky, whom Lester Piggott considered to be the finest of his 30 Classic winners, wins the Derby in 1970

Britain's last Olympic boxing gold medallist, Chris Finnegan, posing for the cameras while out in Mexico in 1968.

James Hunt in his McLaren: A devil-may-care British hero who became Formula One World Champion in 1976.

Jeff Thomson: compacted power released with maximum efficiency.

television, gate receipts and club sponsorship currently falls a very long way short of annual expenditure. For a while that shortfall may be made up by the generous support of wealthy businessman – but not for long and certainly not for ever. The problem is very simple. The top players are being paid inflated salaries and transfer fees and this is spiralling hopelessly out of control.

This has happened in other sports with serious consequences, but fear of failure is driving rugby clubs headlong towards financial ruin. For the big clubs it is essential to be in the First Division, which is where the real money is generated. These clubs receive a fat fee from TV, decent gate receipts and considerable commercial sponsorship. If a club drops to the Second Division, there will immediately be a huge fall in income. To try to ensure continuing First Division status, the top clubs buy players they can not afford and pay salaries they cannot remotely justify. The make-up of the top 24 clubs in England has not altered out of all recognition in the last 50 years but it almost certainly will in the next 50.

If all this sounds rather negative and depressing, let me add quickly that the depression is centred mostly over the heads of the treasurers of the clubs. For the supporters it is a time of immense excitement. A whole host of the world's greatest players have been lured to England, and the general standard of play has improved most significantly with the inevitable extra fitness levels and increased skills that have been derived from full-time professional rugby.

On the other hand, while it is nice to be part of a 15,000 crowd packed into Welford Road to watch Leicester play Saracens with such famous players as South African Springboks Joel Stransky, Fritz van Heerden and Francois Pienaar, Australian Michael Lynagh, Frenchman Phillippe Sella, and Irishman Eric Miller, for clubs outside the top 24 in England plus a few others in Wales not all that much has changed. In the rest of Wales and in almost all Scotland and Ireland the game at club level has not embraced the idea of total professionalism. The top international players in Wales, Scotland and Ireland can probably earn a decent full-time living from playing professional rugby but for 99 per cent very little has changed. All over Britain countless thousands of people play rugby every week for the sheer fun and pleasure they have always derived from a great team game.

The red-faced, pot-bellied extra-B prop forward has not been affected one iota by the International Rugby Board edict on Amateurism in August 1995. For the huge majority of people who have always played for pleasure, nothing has really changed at all. They play for the same healthy reasons that they always played against like-minded opponents and when it is all over after 80 minutes of frantic activity they retire to the bar just as they have always done, sink unconscionable quantities of ale just as they have always done and sing the same old songs just as they have always done.

For that, I breathe a sigh of relief. For every Tiger Woods, it's always nice to know there are a million high handicap rabbits still deriving immense pleasure on golf courses all over the world. Everyone finds and enjoys his own level. And I have taken great heart in the past few months from learning that one of the truly great rugby traditions of the past is not just continuing but positively thriving. I talk of the annual rugby club tour.

In my youth, the rugby club tour was the lifeblood of the game. As every rugby player knows, the annual tour is the focal-point of every season. This event provides enough anecdotes, both macabre and amusing, to act as an anaesthetic, and possibly even as aphrodisiac, during the agony of training twice weekly, and playing every Saturday for the other eight months of the year. The annual tour is a welcome compensation.

In the relatively early days of *Sports Report*, when I was but a callow youth, I went on my first rugby tour with my club side from Edinburgh. As a spotty 17-year-old I was told we would be travelling on a 16-hour coach journey to South Wales, where we would be playing Swansea, Cardiff and Newport in three successive days – something neither the All Blacks nor the Springboks would ever contemplate undertaking.

The pranks which we got up to ranged from the hysterically bizarre to the simply criminal. On my first tour in 1962, I can remember one soberly dressed member of our team, positively exuding respectability in his navy-blue suit, timing his swoop so perfectly that he relieved a station official standing on the platform at Cardiff of both his green flag, with which he was encouraging the departure of the London train, and his peaked cap, which gave him the authority to do so.

Our man then walked solemnly along as much of the train as he could in the 20-minute journey to the next stop at Newport wearing that peaked cap and with his green flag tucked underneath his arm. Those were the good old days of corridor trains, and he went into each compartment and collected all the tickets from the passengers. Having done so, he carefully closed the door of each compartment, and in full view of his immediate victims just as carefully he opened the window in the corridor outside and threw all the tickets he had just collected to the four winds. Each compartment of passengers watched him do this in stunned silence. Not one made a move or said a word. Not one questioned his actions.

Our team duly alighted at Newport, and read with great interest in the newspapers the next day about these hordes of passengers who had arrived at Paddington, all telling the same absolutely preposterous story about why they did not have a valid ticket at the completion of their journey.

It is a rare consolation on my travels round the country to learn that the tour is still an important part of the social calendar and something that every rugby player still looks forward to with a glorious mixture of child-like innocence and Machiavellian duplicity. And after a little research I found further proof, if such proof were necessary, that the end of the world is not nigh. More people not only in Britain but all over the world are playing rugby as amateurs for fun than ever before. Over 70 countries have become affiliated to the governing body, the International Board. Rugby is indisputably booming.

Let the elite enjoy their financial rewards because the remaining 99 per cent of rugby players the world over have their own rich rewards simply from playing a great team game for the sheer pure unadulterated pleasure it brings. Money simply can't buy that – it is a priceless commodity. Perhaps, indeed it is their true love of the game and its characters which explains how the great rugby voices of *Sports Report* down through the past 50 years seem to go on forever.

The incomparable Bill McLaren is as revered and respected now as he was when he first began broadcasting in the early 1950s. Cliff Morgan's mellifluous tones have graced the airwaves in each of the last four decades. It is also true to say that covering rugby for *Sports Report* can give commentators a certain immortality. The wonderful Rex Alston was one of the early original rugby voices way back at the start. Not so very long ago *The Times* published a glowing obituary of Rex, mentioning his lovely turn of phrase and his lively reports, so important and entertaining in those pioneering days of sport on BBC radio.

The Times's obituary editor was therefore rather surprised to receive an irate 'phone call that breakfast-time bitterly complaining about the obituary of Rex Alston. He listened patiently and then inquired if there was one particular aspect to which the caller took exception. The response was not quite what he had anticipated. 'I have just had toast and coffee for breakfast, I am 89 years of age, I am in excellent health and my name is Rex Alston.' Rex pointed out that The Times, as he put it, had made a 'grave' error.

From a rugby angle the ultimate tribute to *Sports Report* is simply that it has attracted so many outstanding rugby reporters to its programme over fifty exciting years. Rex Alston and Bill McLaren go a very long way back. They were joined in the 1960s and 1970s by three redoubtable Welshmen, Cliff Morgan, Alun Williams and David Parry-Jones. In the 1970s and 1980s Peter West was a regular contributor and so too from time to time over the years has been that most outstanding of all rugby writers in the northern hemisphere – Norman Mair, long-time rugby correspondent of the *Scotsman*.

A legend north of the border, Norman Mair is a brilliant wordsmith who has enlivened many a rugby piece for the BBC. It is fitting to give him the final word as *Sports Report* has carried no better piece of descriptive prose in any rugby report in the last 50 years.

In the autumn of 1996 the Australian rugby team left a trail of destruction as they stormed through a 13-match tour unbeaten. It was the most successful tour in the history of Australian rugby this century. You might imagine the coach who was responsible for masterminding this undiluted triumph, Greg Smith, would be in good spirits. Not a bit of it. Not for a moment. In eight weeks in this part of the world, he never smiled. Much worse, he was for ever looking miserable and for ever complaining or so it seemed. The hotels were disappointing, the food was poor, the training pitches inadequate, the refereeing sub-standard, the crowds hostile, the media biased, the weather appalling and so on and so on.

The tabloids wrote of him as a miserable, moaning, whingeing, complaining critical Aussie pain in the back-side. There were several variations on this theme but it was all very basic, uninspiring journalism.

Somehow, we thought, on the eve of the final match, in his own inimitable way, Norman Mair would be able to produce one or two better phrases to describe this rather dour fellow. We were not disappointed. In a trice he captured the essence of the man and summed up the basic characteristics of this introverted and very intense coach. 'Greg Smith, I have to say, does not strike one as your original song and dance man – the sort of person who is likely to be the life and soul of any party.' 'Indeed,' continued Norman, 'he has the aura of one who, if out riding with the four Horsemen of the Apocalypse – Pestilence, Famine, Destruction and Death – would not noticeably alleviate the general mood of the party.'

CLIFF MORGAN

Then and Now

A Welsh fly half of prodigious talents, Cliff Morgan has enjoyed an equally successful career in broadcasting, both as an editor and as presenter for more than ten years of Sport on Four, *as well as many music programmes. Cliff is much in demand as a raconteur and after-dinner speaker.*

Yes, I remember it well. I was just three months away from my 18th birthday on 3 January 1948, when *Sports Report* hit the airwaves on the Light programme at half past five. I was sitting in the kitchen – the back kitchen we called it – of our terraced house at 159 Top Trebanog Road, in a little village that was perched on a hill overlooking the Rhondda Valley in South Wales, where coal had created wealth and misery.

My father sat in silence waiting for this new sports programme and I had just come in from playing football in the Relay Field – the field alongside the house which had a big shed, from which the Welsh Home Service and the Light Programme were relayed to the houses in the valley with its close, encircling hills. My mother was serving up the broth she always made on Saturdays. The cheap-end of lamb, diced vegetables and potato – all fresh from the garden – and a few cubes of Oxo to add some flavour. 'Have you washed your hands?' she said. 'Eat up, and it is best butter on the bread.' Nothing like a mother! For the past fifty years, the signature

tune, 'Out of the Blue', has always prompted thoughts of that
kitchen smell, and lovely it still is.

*Dee-dum, dee-dum, dee-dum, dee-dum, dee-diddly dum
dee-daaah* ... and then the ginny voice of Raymond
Glendenning presenting the show. We loved Glendenning
doing commentary on football and racing. 'He's a Welshman,'
said my dad, 'comes from Newport.' Then came the football
results and my father groaned and then smiled. He was soccer
mad and had captained Trebanog Rovers when they won the
Ely Valley Shield in the 1921-22 season. He waited for the
results of matches played by Cardiff City, Swansea Town,
Newport County and Arsenal. That first day, I remember John
Arlott was reporting on Portsmouth playing Huddersfield
Town and Alan Clarke was at Manchester City. Alan Hoby and
that great newspaper man Peter Wilson talked of sport in the
USA. Little did I know then that years later I would meet and
broadcast with them all on *Sports Report*.

Nothing was outside the range of the programme, for it
appealed to the masses and represented every aspect of
contemporary sport which we all yearned for in those days after
the War. Sporting events were a sell-out and capacity crowds
longed to see the stars who had been lost to them because they
had been on active service. Would Tommy Lawton and Stanley
Matthews be as brilliant as they were before the war? The
youthful Denis Compton had promised so much in the late
1930s, would we be enchanted by his batting again? In 1947
Compton had scored 3,816 runs and 18 centuries and then, as
Sports Report came into being, he played some memorable
innings against Australia followed by the fastest triple century
ever against South Africa. We heard the names of motor racing
first on *Sports Report*. We all wanted to be like Fangio of
Argentina, or Stirling Moss.

During my last year at school in Tonyrefail Grammar, my
English master, Islwyn Evans, insisted that we listened to the
wireless over the weekend and discussed the programmes on the
Monday afternoon. Apart from Dylan Thomas and his *Early
One Morning* – which was rich and noble in its style – we were
advised to listen to the brilliant comedy shows such as *Much*

Binding in the Marsh and *ITMA* and *The Happidrome* with
Tommy Handley – they were the epitome of concise writing and
superb timing. We also had to listen to *Sports Report* for, above
all else, it had good words and successfully incorporated the
surprising line and the classic use of the English idiom. It
understood that the spoken word was so different from the
written word. Reporters had to learn to speak with clarity and
lucidity, and become masters of precis – so vital when reports had
to be exactly one minute and no more. The incomparable David
Coleman, who in his early years was a regular contributor to
Sports Report, once said that 'the man who created it all, Angus
Mackay, built a stop watch into my mind, and right through my
years in broadcasting it has been invaluable.'

I first met David Coleman on *Sports Report* when he was in
Birmingham and I was in Cardiff. Later we worked together on
Grandstand and often spoke of the early days when Angus
Mackay – Mr Mackay as we always called him – taught us the
craft of broadcasting in which you should transmit the feel as
well as the facts. The teachings of *Sports Report* are sculptured
in my mind, after 50 years.

I never cease to talk of the very first time I was interviewed by
Eamonn Andrews on *Sports Report*. Indelibly in my mind is the
Ireland versus Wales rugby international in Dublin. We had just
beaten Ireland and won the Triple Crown, and I was in the bath
and had a terrible pain in my leg. I had broken it (the fibula) and
found it difficult to walk. During the game, Ray Lewis, the
Welsh trainer, had rubbed some oil on my leg and it felt better
and so I finished the game. Then Sammy Walker, who had been
commentating on the match, came to ask if I would be
interviewed by Eamonn Andrews. Much as I loved meeting
Sammy, who had captained the British Lions to South Africa in
1938, I asked to be excused because I couldn't by this time
walk. He went back and reported to Angus Mackay who
simply never took 'No' for an answer. So Sammy was told to get
some help to carry me up the stairs to the commentary box.

That interview I will always remember, for having sought my
opinion of the legendary Irish fly-half, my opposite number
Jack Kyle, Eamonn asked me what I would remember most

about the game. 'My father losing his teeth and he wasn't even playing,' I said. What had happened was that Dad, sitting in probably the worst seat in the grandstand – right on the try line in the one seat we could buy from the Welsh Rugby Union in those days – suddenly had the best seat in the ground. Ken Jones ran some 50 yards at Olympic speed, having worked a scissors movement with me on our 10 yard line, to score – right under my dad. He leapt to his feet and shouted with joy, and spat his top set some twelve rows in front of him. He never got them back! I recall telling this story on Irish Television, and suddenly Tony O'Reilly, the fabulous Irish wing, said: 'Morgan, I know a fella in Cork who is still wearing them!'

This true story is not about the game but about the amusing and unusual things that happen. Hywel Davies, my boss in Wales, had taught me that broadcasting should be about laughter and delight and stories, about pity and gladness, as well as the obligation to give the news and the facts. All in all it was about worthwhileness – games worth reporting, people worth knowing, idiosyncrasies worth noting, players worth looking at and attitudes worth considering. This was the basis of *Sports Report*, which for 50 years has made people smile and wonder. It has brought information and insight, and an enrichment to the audience on a Saturday afternoon, and it is a remarkable experience of sport that will never fade away. Today it marches on with young people who jealously guard the traditions of *Sports Report*, but they also produce even better things than was possible all those years ago.

Eamonn Andrews set a standard of presentation that had a mid-Atlantic swing about it, and it was he who pioneered the 'deaf-aid' which enabled the producer to speak to him during transmission. In fact it was Angus Mackay, a sharp journalist and a canny Scot, who perfected this talkback, for during interviews he would give Eamonn ideas for the next question. It was a powerful combination. Those of us who were fortunate enough to come under the Mackay influence will forever be blessed, for it was he who set the standards in discipline, invention, flair and the importance of checking and then double-checking. Attention to detail was his admirable philosophy.

No one ever refused Angus when they were invited to take part in *Sports Report*. I well remember being in the same waiting room at Broadcasting House as the Duke of Norfolk, Barrington Dalby, John Arlott and J L Manning – all waiting to be ushered into the studio and the probing questions of Eamonn. With Paul Fox, who created *Grandstand* and *Sportsview* on BBC Television, Mackay was a pioneer of sports broadcasting and left us all a glorious legacy. Desmond Lynam, the best television presenter today, cut his teeth in the Mackay stable; as did Alan Parry, Brian Moore, Jim Rosenthal, Chris Martin-Jenkins – and so many other familiar voices.

My close friend Peter Jones, who won a Blue for football at Cambridge, was a favourite of Angus Mackay, for he had words – a vocabulary that was rare and exactly right for every event. One of the finest sports broadcasts in my whole experience was his interview with J L Manning just before he died. In the course of the interview, Manning said:

> Charles Burgess Fry was a fine cricketer who played for Oxford, Sussex and England, held the world long jump record and won an international soccer cap. He missed a rugby blue because of injury, but won a Cup Final medal with Southampton. On top of all that, he was a better scholar than F. E. Smith, who became Lord Chancellor. He was senior scholar to him up at Wadham. He seemed to have an influence on everything and because he came in and out of my house when I was a boy I was greatly impressed by him.

J L Manning's last words were, 'Doesn't all this make us feel terribly humble?'

Humility is what you feel when contributing to *Sports Report*, for at all times you are aware of the greatness that has gone before. It was from Fleet Street that so many of the first fine broadcasters came. Geoffrey Green of *The Times* produced such jewels, week after week. Robin Marlar and the incomparable Harry Carpenter were masters of the spoken word. So too was 'the man they couldn't gag' – Peter Wilson of the *Daily Mirror* who had that acute cutting edge and the ability to make his words and thoughts accessible to all the family as they sat near the wireless. And that, for sure, was the aim of the show when it was created fifty years ago. While Dad listened, pencil poised, to mark his coupon as the football results were read, Angus Mackay knew that to hold the audience the pace and the tempo had to change and very different items were needed to appeal to Mum and the children.

People who were household names in other fields, but had a passion for sport, were interviewed. Richard Burton, the famed actor, confessed on the programme, 'I would rather have played one game for the Welsh rugby team than played Hamlet at the Old Vic.' Spike Milligan revealed his passion for rugby and Ireland. On one programme he said, 'Ciaran Fitzgerald was giving a team talk in the dressing room, and he said, "Right lads, this is a bag, and in it this object, which is a ball." One of the forwards yelled out, "Hold on, you're going too fast for us!"' We listened to the swashbuckling actor, Oliver Reed, talking about his love of boxing and his interest in breeding shire horses. There was Charlton Heston with his love of tennis and Wimbledon in particular. I remember the Welsh novelist, Gwyn Thomas, claiming on the programme: 'I knew a man in Llanelli who cured his shingles by touching the boot of Barry John when that boot was charged with miracles after he'd kicked six goals.' These people gave *Sports Report* that little touch of class which made it a winner for the whole family.

Around the same time as *Sports Report* came on the air, so too did Alistair Cooke with his *Letter From America*. Alistair accepted the invitation to join the show and did so on many occasions. Truly brilliant pieces of broadcasting. He had a passion for golf and the immortal Bobby Jones of America who, in 1930, won what we now call the Grand Slam. He won the American Amateur and the Open and came to these islands to do exactly the same. Alistair claimed that golf was an oasis in a sporting desert of gold and scruffy manners. He quoted a remark made by Bobby Jones: 'Win or lose, the game has no meaning if you don't play by the rules.'

Today, the written word is still so important, and many

distinguished sports writers of what was once Fleet Street keep up those old-fashioned values: Ian Wooldridge, Ken Jones, Patrick Collins, Michael Parkinson, Simon Barnes – and many others. Hugh McIlvanney put into words the feelings of so many when he said that sport was 'a magnificent irrelevance'.

This is the sort of contribution that makes *Sports Report* special. It has respect and admiration for the athletes who enrich our lives – a joy in success and a sympathy in defeat. Furthermore – and this is so vital – the people who make the programme love sport themselves. They believe that you have to take risks and invent, be scorchingly realistic in every situation when you aim to create, and never conspire to destroy.

Ian Payne and John Inverdale tell us that 'It's five o'clock and time for *Sports Report*', and their voices and knowledge of sport are exactly right. These two young men are the face of the programme, but behind them are the engineers without whom all the precious moments are impossible, and the producers who plan and make the show go with a swing. From them comes a storming reminder that it really is a privilege to have 'the best seat in the stand', as Peter Jones always put it, and be able to make people at home feel that they were actually there … although, like me some fifty years ago, they were eating a bowl of broth in the comfort of their home.

In 1954, Angus Mackay and Eamonn Andrews produced a book called *Sports Report*. Mackay wrote then:

> Yes we have the experts, the technicians and a great team spirit. But behind it all lies the unblinking,
> ever-prominent face of a clock in Studio 4A, reminding us that we have just 30 minutes in which to tell our story.

That story has been continuing for a long, long time and I am so proud to have been a tiny part of it for 45 years. *Sports Report* has done well by me and I often ask myself, have I done well by it?

ALAN HOBY

First Edition

*Alan Hoby, for many years Football
Correspondent of the Sunday Express, is the only
surviving contributor to the very first edition of
Sports Report on 3 January 1948, when he gave a
talk on 'Amateurs in Sport'. He still keeps
abreast of the football scene from his
retirement home in Hove.*

I remember Raymond Glendenning, a somewhat portly, friendly man and one of the authentic voices of sports radio. Peter Wilson, an Old Harrovian and ardent Socialist with a splendid moustache, was *the* popular *Sunday* and later *Daily Mirror* sports columnist – 'The Man They Can't Gag', the *Mirror* called him. He was a great boxing writer in the days before television took over. He had a penchant for the theatrical and wore expensive suits with double-breasted waistcoats, sometimes sported (quite illegally) a swordstick and was even known to wear a Glencarry cape and Sherlock Holmes hat. He was a great extrovert and drinker (when not on the job) with a pungent and pithy style – for example, 'he had a chest like a busted mattress' to describe the hulking Jake La Motta (Robert de Niro played him later in a movie) during his losing fight with probably the best middleweight in modern times, Sugar Ray Robinson.

Charles Buchan, a former Arsenal and England football great, was another Angus Mackay regular who wrote about the game with professional authority. A very straight man, highly respected and a founder-member of the now thriving and powerful Football Writers' Association. He must be kicking his grave at some of the overpaid, Gazza-type prima donnas infesting the game today...

My own memories of *Sports Report* are of the *rush* (by taxi or underground) from the big London grounds to Portland Place. The matches ended around 4.40 to 4.45pm and you had to get to the studio well before the 5.30pm deadline if humanly possible. With huge crowds leaving the grounds, often before the end, split-second timing (and writing!) was essential: trying to please editors, readers, listeners, and yourself and catching all the deadlines meant there was a tight-rope excitement about everything.

MAGIC MOMENTS...

Cricket correspondent Jonathan Agnew fell victim to that affliction called 'Broadcaster's Mouth' when filing a report about a TCCB inquiry.

He said: 'The authorities found that Lamb had made a deliberate and fragrant breach of regulations.'

JAMES ALEXANDER GORDON

East Fife 4 Forfar 5

*James Alexander Gordon has been reading
the classified football results on Sports Report for
half of the programme's 50-year history.
Here he reveals his own career in football and the
perks of his present job.*

My earliest recollection of taking part in sport was when I was
about twelve. Most of my friends played football in the street,
using jackets and jumpers as goal posts. I had had polio and was
weighed down with bulky leg irons, but this did not deter me
from taking part. At worst, I could be a corner flag with a
hankie in my mouth. As a player, goalkeeper was deemed the
only position suitable for me. The jumpers and jackets would
be moved in a bit so that if the ball came my way I could simply
fall on it. Should a high shot be fired at me be over arms length,
the opposing team had scored. It's a tough game, football!

The radio was all we had to keep up with sports events and it
was while listening to the football results I said to my Dad, 'I'd
like to do that'. Little did he know that, twenty-five years on, I
would be that man in *Sports Report*.

Over the years I've had some fabulous mail. Some people
write regularly, some are amusing. A Bank manager from
Nigeria wrote to ask if I could guarantee eight draws a week
assuring me of ten percent of the winnings. A Saudi Prince

wrote of his passion for the game and said that listening to the results had helped him with his English! On holiday in Crete a chap told me he listened to me every week in Perth. 'Ah,' I said, 'a fellow Scot'? 'No', he replied with what was not a Scottish accent. Perth Australia. One Saturday, while driving into London I was stopped for speeding. I explained to the officer that I was on my way to read the football results. 'I suppose you think you're James Alexander Gordon?' 'I am', I said, showing him my licence. With a stern warning I was on my way to Broadcasting House. The great thing for me in being involved with *Sports Report* is being part of a fantastic team. Even after twenty five years I still get a buzz when the signature tune strikes up and still think, when I read the classified results that the microphone is one person, the listener.

STUART HALL

A Visit to Oakwell

One of Sports Report's *longest-serving reporters
and undoubtedly the most idiosyncratic, Stuart
Hall escapes from his Wilmslow fastness on
Saturday afternoons to patrol the northern
footballing outposts. In his youth he played the
Victoria Palace himself – he was on the books of
Crystal Palace.*

Barnsley is onomatopoeic. It is what it is and e'er will be. Steel, iron, coal, Scargill, tough as teak, Yorkshire.

Not having visited Oakwell for a quarter of a century, I was despatched there to witness Barnsley's joust with Birmingham City on their triumphal progress to the promised land of the Premiership. Oakwell is not easy to find. I wandered lonely as a cloud o'er hills and dales until I found Pattpong Road (or similarly y'clept). Driving the Huppmobile down it I turned into yet another steep decline at the end of which stood a posse of rubicund Yorkist bobbies. What's the collective noun for policemen? Fandango of fuzz, cornucopia of coppers, plumage of police? 'Can't park here sunshine,' observed a large bluebottle with a choirboy's visage. I abandoned the Huppmobile on high ground for fear of locusts. ''Ast tha' gotten a pass?' 'No,' I replied. 'I'm with the BBC.' Gate forty twoooo. Ah'll tek thee.' Dying for a leak, I dived into a urinal straight from Jacques Tati's Clochmerle Pop Gothic. I began to laugh – this is football as it should be. I felt at home – after a Pop Gothic pee.

To the press box, cheek by jowl with the audience. The charladies had been a trifle lax. The odd chip paper, sweet wrapper, gobbets of dust blown in on the Yorkshire Mistral. The ground is atop a hill and the wind blew fierce this day. I had come to witness Barnsley's Brazilian Blend football and to pay homage to Danny Wilson, a wonderful wing half of his day. I laughed a lot. Rustic gaiety. Here at Oakwell amid Brazilian footie and flat Yorkshire vowels lie the grassroots of the beautiful game.

Alas, the plot went awry. With the gale at his back, the Birmingham full back blasted a 60-yard kick through the Barnsley net and into Grimethorpe Colliery. Blow wind and cataract. Barnsley's poise evaporated and Birmingham did the business. One-nowt to Brum.

Afterwards I mused with Danny Wilson, an open-faced lad of the soil, an honest, straight gent. He loved the fact that I'd loved the day. A tight, spruce, little ground. A board of directors brewed locally. A fans' football club. We chuckled and relished the thought of Chelsea's stretch limo crawling down Pattpong Road. Ken Bates and his sophisticated cronies incredulous. Le Boeuf, Di Matteo, Emile Zola, Vialli and Rude singing 'Waters over Troubled Bridge'. (Apologies to Simon and Garfunkel.) Those pansy yellow and blue pyjamas that Chelsea sport heckled off the pitch.

From San Siro to Oakwell. From larks' tongues in aspic with quail eggs, to baked beans and Bovril. It's Don Quixote time, I love it. Romance lives in Barnsley.

In Praise of Bob Paisley

In 1977 Liverpool were poised for a unique treble. League Championship. FA Cup. European Cup. Herewith, the story of the most thrilling day of my life.

Liverpool lost to Manchester United in the F.A. Cup. Won the Championship. But, four days after the Wembley debacle had to play Borussia Moenchengladbach in Rome. A multitude of

Scousers made the trek. By land, sea, air. Hitch-hiking, back-packing, foot-slogging, sleeping where they could. The glory of Rome spurred them on. Dreams and the light imaginings of men, of all that faith creates and love desires. Rome, the Eternal City. The cradle of civilisation. This was not simply a football match, it was a distillation of people's lives crystallised into 90 minutes.

I persuaded the BBC to commit all its resources to the occasion. Film crews recorded it all. Rome was a sea of red and white. Thousands of fans invaded the Vatican. Played football in St Peter's Square, asked the Pope for spare tickets. Took over the bars. Knew the prices of everything from cafe to concierges, pasta to prostitutes. Rome embraced this vociferous, friendly invasion. Humour flowed. Carabinieri unemployed.

The focal point was the Liverpool dressing room. Bob Paisley had agreed that I could film everything from start to finish. An honest son of Bishop Auckland. A steadfast wing half. A servant of the cause.

The morning before the match I had no passes for the match. Peter Robinson thus loaded into a taxi a bootful of silver plate to grease the palms of FIFA. We set off for HQ deadline 1 p.m. Tuesday. Half-way down the Via Veneto we stopped at traffic lights. Suddenly a lorry crashed into the back of the taxi. Our driver decamped to remonstrate. *'Multo cativo basta basta'*, plus a stream of Roman invective. Then – armed Carabinieri alighted from the lorry, not pleased. I apologised to them for reversing up the Via Veneto. Obtained a crowbar. Bashed the boot open. Transferred the silver to another cab. Arrived breathless and faint at FIFA HQ. Hans and Co. acquired the silver, and smilingly parted with all the passes.

Suddenly there entered Gigi Peronace, the head of Italy's football mafia. Black hair greased back, bespoke suit, Gucci shoes, mohair coat slung casually over his shoulders. *'Che fato alora'*. He casually ripped up my tickets. *'Solo Italiano en stadio. Impossibili.'* Peter, that smashing bloke, was stunned. I was poleaxed. I'd committed the BBC to vast expenditure for nothing. Back at the Liverpool hotel the players were relaxing. Players see nothing of the world, only the training ground and their digs. Bob Paisley, that granite man was sympathetic.

Leave it to me he whispered in that mellifluous Durham burr.

Two hours before the match I boarded the Liverpool coach. Kevin Keegan secreted the camera. Tommy Smith the lighting rig, Steve Heighway the microphones, Phil Neal assorted paraphernalia. We all wore Liverpool tracksuits. Escorted by a wailing police escort we were wafted into the Olympic Stadium, straight through the portals unchallenged.

The dressing-rooms are in Michelangelo marble. Vastly imposing. I locked my camera crew in the lavatories to escape marauding Italian officials. T'was a big mistake. The players on the eve of their biggest day suffered evacuation of the bowel syndrome. And there was no running water in the bogs. Italians were everywhere smelling a rat! Bob Paisley said 'Walk round the ground – take the escort with you.' I strolled into the May sunshine. The stadium a cradle of cacophony, a mass of red and white, banners, flags, scarves. A non-stop din of music and chants. The nape hairs stood on end. Did Christians experience this 2000 years ago?

I returned to the dressing room. The doors were closed. Lights on, cameras whirred. Kevin Keegan nursing two black eyes, courtesy of Jimmy Case. (Kevin was leaving for Hamburg.) Terry McDermott the joker, Emlyn Hughes singing. Time to leave. Suddenly, all the players drummed their boots on the marble floor. A battlecry. The drumming rose to a crescendo. The Charge of the Light Brigade. The hooves, the cries, do or die. The atmosphere charged like a storm over the Himalayas. Two great teams. England versus Germany. Clemence, Neal, Jones, Hughes, Smith, Case, Kennedy, Callaghan, McDermott, Keegan, Heighway. As we left Bob asked me where I was going to sit. I shrugged. 'You are one of the subs' he said. So I locked dressing room one with the key and trotted out with Toshack, Thompson and Co.

I sat on that bench transfixed like a rabbit with the stoat on it. Keegan was electric. At the top of his form. Shadowed by Berti Vogts. Vogts pummelled Kev black and blue, rabbit punches, slaps, nudges, gross fouls, Kev's shirt pulled off his back. Borussia with great names Stielike, Simonsen, Vogts himself. Epic football. Epic atmosphere. Stielike, hurt, rolled over the touchline. A screaming diatribe of Scouser abuse from our bench had him hurtling back on the pitch. Then Heighway with that high stepping impala gait threaded through a pass, McDermott in full cry from midfield hit a super goal. Half-time one-nil to Liverpool. I galloped back to our dressing room. 'Roll the cameras, we're one up.' The players rushed in. Excitement, fulfilment of hopes, the ultimate achievement. Bob Paisley cossetted each one gently in praise. His style was consummate. A blueprint for man management.

Second half was almost a blur. First Simonsen beat Clemence in a top corner of Clem's net. One apiece. Steve Heighway hit a spectacular corner. Tommy Smith leonine as ever on it, a header among the flying boots of Borussia – Liverpool in the lead. Kevin Keegan by now mangled by Vogts bore down on goal. The Borussia keeper mesmerised. Vogts, the shadow, fouled Kev – penalty. Phil Neal stepped forward. He'd rehearsed this penalty kick a thousand times. Borussia's keeper 6 feet 3 inches. Keep it low. Just inside the post. Thus it was. Brilliant pen. 3–1. Game and pride. I never saw Emlyn Hughes take the trophy. I sprinted for the dressing rooms. As I was unlocking the door Borussia's players, some in tears, clattered down the marble halls bearing their green and white jerseys.

They proferred them. I refused, mumbling I was BBC. Liverpool arrived at last after laps of the stadium in delirium. Strangely, celebrations were muted, underplayed, as if this momentous occasion was part of their destiny, a nemesis. Joviality was confined to the showers. Amid the steam, the heat, the lights, the celebration through the open door stepped Gigi Peronace, smooth, oily, arrogant as ever. Suddenly he took in the whole scene. His jaw literally dropped. He was speechless. Beside himself with rage. We'd beaten his system. He couldn't fathom how. For us Brits the word *'impossibili'* doesn't exist. He turned on his heel and departed. Without a word. The players melted into the night.

On upturned skips sat Bob Paisley, Ronnie Moran, Joe Fagan, Roy Evans, Tom Saunders and me. Drinking warm Coca Cola from polystyrene cups. No Krug or Moet. No lead crystal. Bob smiled his coal miner's smile. 'This is the second time I've conquered Rome. The first was driving a tank in World War Two.' We rose. I said 'I must go seek some dew drops here. And hang a pearl in every cowslip's ear.' I closed the door. Liverpool had left their mark, in more ways than one, on Rome. I still have the key. A constant reminder of Bob, his bootroom boys, Peter Robinson, and the staff of the greatest football club in the world.

CHRISTINE JANES
with Joanne Watson

Wimbledon Memories

A former French Open champion and singles finalist at Wimbledon, where her flowing style and impeccable court manners made her a great favourite with the crowd, Christine Janes (née Truman) has been part of the BBC Radio commentary team since 1975.

I suppose it was inevitable that I should become a tennis player. My parents had met at the local tennis club and they would recall how they'd seen the legendary French champion Suzanne Lenglen at Wimbledon. I didn't start playing properly until I was 10 and then I had just half an hour's coaching every two or three weeks with Herbert Brown, the Essex coach. However it was enough for me to set my heart on wanting to be a Wightman Cup player and play at Wimbledon.

In those days we didn't have a television so I hadn't seen the Championships, but my family always followed tennis through the papers and on the radio and when I was 12 I was allowed to go to Wimbledon with two school friends on the middle Saturday. I know we were all very excited as we got on the train at Woodford and arrived early to queue for tickets for Court 2. The first match I remember was a doubles between the Italian pair of Orlando Sirola and Nikki Pietrangeli and we became big fans. We then waited for any return tickets for Centre or

Number 1 Court and got home after nine. Sadly I can't imagine many parents letting children of that age make such a trip unaccompanied nowadays.

Four years later I was playing at the Championships myself. Although I'd qualified to play at fifteen, the minimum age limit was sixteen, as it is now. I'd practised at Wimbledon for several years with Dan Maskell, the LTA coach, and I'd even walked on the Centre Court with him, so I didn't feel intimidated. But I don't think even he could have imagined that I'd reach the semi-finals in my first year. I did have an amazing confidence and belief which comes with youth, that if I entered a tournament I could possibly win it. It's like the young people of today, you don't think of the ifs and buts, you just go for it.

I had a shaky couple of matches in the early rounds, but what made my name was when I beat the French Champion, Shirley Bloomer, also of Britain. The match, on the first Saturday, was on Number 1 Court, and it was just one of those days when I hit a purple patch and everything went in. From then on my life changed. My family were staggered by all the press interest. I remember sitting round the breakfast table on the Sunday morning reading all the reports and having my leg pulled, it all seemed unreal. Suddenly our Essex garden was full of photographers taking pictures. Incidentally my father had missed the match because he was the treasurer of the local church and the annual fete had taken priority!

Then I beat Betty Pratt of the USA in the quarters, which took me through to the semi-finals against another American, Althea Gibson. Frankly I didn't play well and she played very well and went on to win the title. However, I was thrilled to be invited into the Royal Box for tea by the then Duchess of Kent, Princess Marina. The Yorkshire and England cricketer Freddie Trueman sent me a bunch of white roses and I received my first telegram from Winston Churchill, my local MP. I can remember the great rivalry between the locker rooms; I was in the no. 3 room while all the seeds were in the no. 1 locker room, and all my fellow unknowns were cheering me on against the established stars. Although teenage players are almost the norm in the women's game today, my youth made me an exception in the late 1950s, which is partly why I received so much attention. Because I was so tall, nearly 6 feet, I had the height and strength to compete in the senior game.

Although I was disappointed to lose to Althea, the following year I did gain some revenge, beating her in the Wightman Cup on Number 1 Court. This competition was played between the women of Britain and the United States and featured the country's best players. The Cup was competed for every other year, and when it was staged in Britain it was held at Wimbledon, the week before the Championships. I'd been coached specifically to combat Gibson's high bouncing top spin serve, one of her best weapons, and for weeks I'd practised receiving them so when I came to play her it wasn't the dangerous shot it might have been. One thing that impressed me about her was how sporting she was when she lost. Although we won the Cup that year, British victories were few and far between and the Wightman Cup was eventually shelved because Britain just couldn't compete on level terms.

The emotional and inspirational matches are one aspect of Wimbledon that appeals to spectators and makes it so special. The first final I saw, in 1954, was such a match. It featured Jaroslav Drobny, the Czech refugee and former Olympic ice hockey medallist, and Australian Ken Rosewall. It was Drobny's 11th Championship, and here he was at 32 and no one thought he'd win. It just shows no matter how many times you lose you've always got a chance, and that's why youngsters should always go and watch and see what can happen. Ironically, Rosewall, the favourite then, never won the title, losing three other finals. There were similar emotions in 1997 when Jana Novotna reached her second final against the 16-year-old Martina Hingis. Novotna had lost the 1993 final against Steffi Graf when on the brink of victory, and had then burst into tears on the Duchess of Kent's shoulder at the presentation. This time she was the sentimental favourite. People said it was Jana's turn but it doesn't happen like that. I think I've learnt that life never goes in a straight pattern as neat and tidy as you plan. It often takes a turn, not always because of something horrid, sometimes for quite pleasant reasons.

I can empathise with Jana, because in 1961 I came close to winning the Championship. Having beaten the Number 1 seed Margaret Smith (Court) from match point down in the quarter finals, I went on to reach the final against another British player, Angela Mortimer. However, fate took a hand, and when I was leading by a set and 4–3 I turned to chase a lob and fell awkwardly. In those days there was no such thing as an injury time out, not even a chair to sit down on at the changeover, and Angela seized her chance to take the title. Strangely, my real sense of disappointment didn't hit me until I was at the Wimbledon Ball. By tradition the women's and men's champions always started the dancing, and that's what I'd always dreamt of doing. After the speeches I felt the let down terribly, but I suppose I thought that next time I'd be back and doing that. However life isn't quite that simple!

After I'd finished playing, BBC Radio asked me if I'd like to try my hand at commentating, so I went down to Eastbourne and 22 years later I'm still trying!

I've been fortunate to have seen many great matches at Wimbledon and one of the most emotional was the 1977 women's final when Virginia Wade won the title in Jubilee year, when the Queen made her only visit to a final.

Virginia was a bit of a Novotna, she had the game and the talent but never quite seemed able to sustain it through a tournament. Year after year the crowds had witnessed the nailbiting ups and downs of Virginia's career, but in 1977, when she was nearly 32, she at last achieved what the public had yearned for. In fact Britain had two of the top four seeds that year, with Sue Barker reckoned as the more likely finalist of the two. She played Betty Stove while Virginia took on the Number 1 seed Chris Evert. That was probably Virginia's best match, but the public were denied an all-British final when Barker lost.

The final wasn't a great spectacle. Virginia and the crowd were all rather nervy, but it was as if fate had decreed. I think that to win the title in front of the Queen must have been the ultimate dream . Spare a thought, though, for Betty Stove, she reached three finals that year and lost them all.

Sometimes finals can be gripping even if the tennis isn't of the highest quality. Margaret Court against Billie Jean King in 1970 wasn't, by King's own admission, a great match for the tennis purists even though they were probably the world's two best players. Both were far from fully fit but Court won 14–12 11–9 in a tremendous encounter.

On many occasions finals haven't lived up to expectations because one player has played too well, but in 1980 John McEnroe and Bjorn Borg staged a truly memorable match. The highlight was a 4th-set tie break that went for nearly 20 minutes with set and match points being almost equally distributed. McEnroe won it 18–16, but Borg took the final set and his fifth successive title. McEnroe was one of the most gifted players Wimbledon has ever seen, and probably the most temperamental. Borg, on the other hand, was ice cool and reigned supreme on both clay and grass. His trade mark bandana and long hair made him the first teenybop hero. That tie break was riveting, with some amazing shot play and both men playing well at the same time, which doesn't happen too often. It was the sort of match you always hope for as a spectator when you buy your tickets.

McEnroe gained his revenge the following year to win the first of his three titles, but he will, of course, be as much remembered for his behaviour as his tennis. His infamous berating of an umpire during one match on Number 1 court, calling him the 'pits of the world' brought a new expression into the language. Behaviour on court changed with him and suddenly impressionable people felt they had to behave like that to play well. It was always a little bit worrying when he lost his temper, but since he's gone that element has faded.

At the other extreme was Chris Evert, who was champion three times. She was known as the Ice Maiden, and although she never showed any emotion she was a great competitor. I saw her win numerous games from game point down. What made her such a great player was that she never let a point slip, and that was part of the secret of her success. I empathised with Evert, since I was taught never to show any emotion on court by my mother. She was very strict and would watch all my matches. There were times in my early playing days when I felt

I would be sent to bed if I misbehaved – I only wished I had the same effect on my children. I imagine she would have been horrified by Boris Becker's tormented rantings or the antics of the likes of Illie Nastase or Jimmy Connors.

Of course Wimbledon has been the perfect stage for the star performers. Maria Bueno, the talented Brazilian champion,exuded film-star quality in her personality and appearance and had the talent to match. She would play dramatic shots when ordinary shots would do – they weren't for the crowd, they were for herself.

That era was one in which fashion played its part. Teddy Tinling, the legendary dress designer, would create stunning individual outfits for the star players which were all the more effective because you couldn't go and buy something similar in the shops. Those were the days when the best dressed players would come on court in dress and cardigan, and I know I would spend hours picking out mine. I had two favourites, a pale pink and pale blue! Any one who saw Virginia's final will remember her bright pink cardy. These days there's not a cardy in sight on Centre Court. I wonder why not!

Of course not all the thrilling matches are in the finals. There was the epic five-hour marathon between Pancho Gonzales and Charlie Pasarell in the pre-tie-break days of 1969. It seemed to go on for days and set a record of 112 games. There were the innumerable five-setters with Borg, and the time Neale Fraser beat Earl 'Butch' Buchholz when he collapsed with cramp at 15 games all in the fourth set of their quarter final. Buchholz had no fewer than six match points, but Fraser went on to win the title.

Of course the crowd can play its part. In my early days it was more genteel and sedate, but a great inspiration none the less; nowadays it's more vociferous. I was pleased to hear that Tim Henman and Greg Rusedski both said how much the crowd helped them. I hope the days are gone when British players think it imposes too much pressure on them.

The end of my playing career heralded a new era and one of the modern greats, Martina Navratilova. We met in the first round. I knew it was a tough draw because everyone said how amazing this young player was and indeed so she proved, winning the singles title nine times. Of the current players I have a great admiration for Steffi Graf. Her pre-eminence comes from her terrific athleticism and bullet-like forehand. Modern players like the same pace, but Graf has a powerful forehand and a slice backhand so it upsets her opponents, and of course she has a marvellous temperament. To be a Wimbledon champion that's essential, otherwise you couldn't cope. Hingis has got it, Seles had it before the stabbing. I think it's something you're partly born with, and Wimbledon certainly finds out the players who have the talent but aren't tough enough mentally to get through.

Among the men, I still rate Rod Laver as the best. He was champion four times, and would probably have won the title more times had he not turned professional at the height of his powers, and become ineligible to play. I very nearly played mixed doubles at Wimbledon with him until my mother intervened. She reminded me that I'd agreed to play with my brother and no matter how good Laver was I couldn't change partners! Laver was part of Harry Hopman's group which produced a string of great players. Fraser, Hoad, Rosewall, Newcombe, Stolle and Emerson were part of this Australian contingent who took on and beat the world. In a 16-year period Australians won the title 13 times, often beating other Aussies in the final!

The memorable matches and great players are almost too numerous to mention. Every year there seems to be another match to add to the illustrious catalogue. The People's Sundays have been successful if tiring additions, and the new Number 1 court immediately made a positive impact.

One man who was very much a part of Wimbledon and BBC Radio history was Fred Perry. Champion three times in the 1930s and doyen of the Davis Cup team before turning professional, Fred was a giant of the game. Despite his age he travelled the world and never lost his enthusiasm for keeping up with the modern game. He understood what had changed and the expectations and pressures on the current players. He never said things were better in his day, but because he'd been through it at this level he was revered by the modern stars who could never have seen him play. In just a few words he could pinpoint precisely where a player was going wrong or right.

Of course Wimbledon has changed a lot since Fred's day, particularly on the money side. For my losing final I received a voucher for £15, the winner got just £20. In 1997 the women's champion received £373,000. Some people say the pressure is greater on today's players, but I only hope they're doing what they enjoy.

Wimbledon has moved with the times like other major events, and I know people who come here only occasionally and can't believe the changes that the club has gone through. Of course, the Championships have had their hiccups. The boycott years of 1972 and 1973 when most of the leading male players didn't play threatened the institution. But the Championships have remained a favourite with players and spectators alike. Some things never alter, the strawberries and cream, the Virginia Creeper, the vagaries of the British weather and above all the special aura of the All England Club which for me make it unsurpassable. Even out of season it has a special something that makes you feel all the better for going.

ALAN PARRY

A Learning Experience

Football commentator Alan Parry is one of a
number of current television broadcasters who
learned their craft on Sports Report. *Alan, who*
also commentates on athletics, is a director of
Wycombe Wanderers FC.

Whatever I do in the rest of my broadcasting career, it can never compare with the excitement of my first appearance on *Sports Report*. The famous 'Five O'Clock Show' has been an important part of my life for as long as I can remember.

In the days when I was growing up in the suburbs of Liverpool in the 1950s, the 'wireless' was the main form of entertainment. I spent countless hours listening to the exciting commentaries of Raymond Glendenning and the silky Irish tones of Eamonn Andrews. Like most kids on Merseyside in those days, I had dreams of being a footballer myself. All the young lads in the street where I lived would listen to the radio football commentary then rush out to play, pretending to be the stars they had just been hearing about. Radio gave us the chance to dream.

When reality set in and I knew that I wasn't going to earn a living by kicking a ball, I became even more interested in the world of broadcasting. I began to take more notice of those famous radio voices, their different styles and accents. Journalism was always my chosen profession once the dream of being a footballer had faded. I left school and started work as a junior reporter on my local newspaper, the *Liverpool Weekly News*. Wherever the paper sent me on a Saturday afternoon, I made sure that I was always near a radio at five o'clock. I loved the world of newspapers, but even in those days my thoughts were turning to broadcasting as a possible future career. I would marvel at the skills of legendary radio reporters like Bill Bothwell, Alan Clarke, Maurice Edelston, Larry Canning and the incomparable Peter Jones.

My big break came when BBC Radio Merseyside started broadcasting. At the time I was working for a news agency in Liverpool and we were given the contract to supply the new station with its coverage of news and sport. At first that meant just writing the bulletins, but my chance to broadcast soon came about. Within a few months of my debut in front of the microphone I was asked to do a match report for BBC Radio Two. The game was Oxford United v Liverpool in the third round of the FA Cup in season 1971-72. Then, as now, *Sports Report* covered as many third-round ties as possible, and when they were unable to send their own correspondent they would use a reporter from the local radio station.

That's how my *Sports Report* debut came about. I covered most of Liverpool's away games for Radio Merseyside and there was a great deal of interest in this tie. Liverpool – as usual! – were going well near the top of the league, but a visit to the sloping pitch of second division Oxford was seen as a potentially tricky tie. As it turned out, the Liverpool players were far more confident about the game than a nervous young reporter was about appearing on *Sports Report*. Bill Shankly's team romped to an easy 3–0 victory with Kevin Keegan scoring twice while I sat in the press box fretting and agonising over every word of my report.

When my big moment came and presenter Des Lynam uttered the words: 'Our reporter at the Manor Ground is Alan Parry...' I was frozen with fear. For me, this was like playing up front for Liverpool and if I got it wrong I might never be picked again. Exactly sixty seconds later – it had to be *exactly* with Angus Mackay in charge of the programme – it was all over and Des had moved on to the next match report. How did it sound?

Well, that was the question I fired at dozens of friends and relatives who I had instructed to listen in. Some forgot, a few were complimentary and most said: 'Oh, it was okay I suppose'. I wonder if the recording still exists? I can't have been too awful, because within eighteen months I got the call to join the *Sports Report* team in London as a full time member of staff. It was a great thrill for me to join a team which included Des Lynam, Peter Jones, Maurice Edelston, Bryon Butler and many other broadcasting legends.

In ten years with BBC Radio I went on to present *Sports Report* many times and the feeling of excitement as the clock ticked towards 5.00pm and the start of that famous signature tune never left me. To this day, five o'clock on a Saturday afternoon means only one thing.

I was fortunate enough to work under the inventor of *Sports Report*, the legendary and fearsome Angus Mackay, for my first few months before Angus retired. What a character. What a man. His discipline was very strict, and if he asked you to deliver a one minute report it had to be just that – one minute. Fifty-nine seconds or sixty-one seconds and you were in deep trouble. Angus created the feeling that you were privileged to appear on *Sports Report* – and he was right. The greatest names in sport would happily drop everything to come on to the show. It was a very special invitation which no one ever refused.

I had some great moments. Crossing verbal swords with feisty football managers whose teams had just been beaten; transatlantic 'phone calls to Muhammad Ali; chairing topical debates with Fleet Street greats like J. L. Manning and Peter Wilson. We would be live on air for four and a half hours every Saturday, but it was the sixty minutes between five and six o'clock that really mattered. To millions of people sitting in the comfort of their homes or returning from sporting events it was – and still is – *Sports Report* which is first with the news.

Naturally, in ten years' close association with the programme there were many memorable moments. Great games, big stories, riveting interviews. But the greatest memory of all concerns a day when it all went horribly wrong. In the mid-1970s, the draw for the third round of the FA Cup – which had traditionally been made on Radio Two at midday on Monday – was switched to television and a Saturday afternoon slot live on *Grandstand*. The idea was that *Sports Report* would join *Grandstand* for the draw and then return to the radio studio in Broadcasting House for the rest of the programme. It was always the practice to repeat the draw for those who had missed a particular team the first time round.

As the presenter that day, I pointed out that it would be too difficult for me to scribble down every tie in legible fashion in time to instantly repeat the draw on air. It was decided that one of the backroom team, a wonderful character called Godfrey 'Goddo' Dixey, would help me. 'Goddo's' brainwave was to write the name of every team involved in the third round draw on to sticky jam jar labels which he could place in order as the draw was taking place. Perfect.

It all began smoothly enough. The voice from Lancaster Gate intoned: 'Number 26 – Arsenal – will play number 8 – Coventry City'. And 'Goddo' duly tore of the respective labels for Arsenal and Coventry and stuck them alongside each other on a virginal sheet of white paper.

Unfortunately, the officials at FA headquarters got a little carried away by the thought of appearing on television and took far too long to make the early part of the draw. They were instructed to move at a faster pace – with disastrous consequences for yours truly back in the *Sports Report* studio. As the draw speeded up, dear old 'Goddo' got more and more agitated. Soon, his sticky labels began to tear in half and his neat white paper looked as though it had been out in the rain. I could read 'Arsenal v Coventry', but what was I supposed to make of '...cester City v ... Wanderers'? Or '...port Count... v ... United'? Poor 'Goddo' began to panic and I was consumed by a fit of the giggles. The end of the draw was approaching and the jumble of names and stray letters in front of me looked like a message from outer space!

Somehow I stumbled through the repeat of the third round draw, but it bore no similarity to the real thing. Leeds fans must have been cursing their luck at being drawn away to Everton when in fact they were at home to Darlington! I just hope the recording of that show doesn't remain in the archives.

Despite the very mention of the day sending an icy shiver down my spine, *Sports Report* remains my favourite programme of the week on radio or television. Angus Mackay was right when he said it was a privilege to appear on the best sports programme of them all.

In Memoriam
Peter Jones

On Saturday 15 April 1989, 96 football fans lost their lives at Hillsborough, venue of the FA Cup semi-final between Liverpool and Nottingham Forest. It was the worst tragedy in British sporting history, and had a far-reaching effect on both the design of football grounds and the future conduct of the game.
Peter Jones, the BBC's senior commentator, was there. He delivered this report, live and unscripted, at the top of Sports Report.

Well, I think the biggest irony is that the sun is shining now, and Hillsborough's quiet, and over there to the left the green Yorkshire hills, and who would have known that 74 people would die here in the stadium this afternoon.

I don't necessarily want to reflect on Heysel, but I was there that night broadcasting with Emlyn Hughes, and he was sitting behind me this afternoon, and after half an hour of watching stretchers going out and oxygen cylinders being brought in and ambulance sirens screaming, he touched me on the shoulder and he said, 'I can't take any more.' And Emlyn Hughes left. And two other items I just think of sitting here now in the sunshine that still remind me of Heysel – the gymnasium here at Hillsborough is being used as a mortuary for the dead, and at this moment stewards, just as they did at the Heysel stadium, have got cartons and little paper bags and they're gathering up the personal belongings of the spectators, some of whom died, some of whom are now seriously injured in nearby hospitals.

And there are red and white scarves of Liverpool, and red and white bobble hats of Liverpool and red and white rosettes of Liverpool, and nothing else out there on the enclosure where all the deaths occurred. And the sun shines now.

Peter Jones collapsed while delivering commentary on the 1990 Boat Race, and died 36 hours later without regaining consciousness. JON CHAMPION was presenting Sport On Two *and* Sports Report *for the first time that day.*

Walking out through the grand portals of Broadcasting House on the evening of Saturday 31 March 1990 should have been a satisfying experience. After a five-hour stint in studio B9, it was time to face the world after my debut as presenter of *Sport on Two* and *Sports Report*, but the world wasn't ready to be faced. The streets of Central London were near-deserted, sealed off to traffic after that afternoon's violent protests against the poll tax; sirens wailed in the distance, and a cold wind sent litter scattering in all directions. The feeling of emptiness was overwhelming, yet it owed little to the eerie scene.

Those of us who had worked on the programme gathered, as usual, in the BBC Club for what should have been a jolly debriefing. However the mood was sombre and there was but one topic of conversation. Peter Jones, a doyen among sports broadcasters, had started the afternoon by setting the scene from the banks of the Thames; now, a few hours later, he was lying gravely ill in hospital after suffering a massive heart attack whilst commentating on the Boat Race. It would be another 36 hours before Peter's death was announced, but those present were somehow already in mourning.

It was all a world apart from the previous afternoon when Peter, typically dapper in blazer and flannels and carrying the obligatory pile of books under his arm, had wished a nervous novice well in the Sportsroom. ''Just enjoy it – you'll be fine,' was the gist of his advice. Easy to say, hard to follow, I thought, but nice of him to say anything at all.

That next day, I recall handing over to Peter prior to the race, and feeling glad of the respite it provided a debutant presenter … twenty minutes to gather one's thoughts. Peter was on the BBC Radio launch behind the two crews, but all too quickly his speech began to falter and, without explanation, the voice of summariser Dan Topolski took over. Glances were exchanged through the glass of the studio window – word rapidly came that the BBC's senior commentator had collapsed. While Robert Treharne-Jones, a doctor, did what he could on board, somehow Topolski completed the commentary, an achievement overshadowed by the circumstances.

So often for listeners of my generation, the lead item on *Sports Report* had been a report from Peter Jones. That evening, the man who had described the news so vividly was the subject of the news. It was far from easy to complete the programme: 'Out of the Blue' carried a deep poignancy that night.

MAGIC MOMENTS…

BBC Sports Correspondent Adam Mynott slipped up during a report about security measures being organised in Belgium for the arrival of English fans for a European Cup tie.

When asked how tough the local security forces would be on potential miscreants, Mynott replied: 'Well, it's clear that Belgian Police will take no prisoners…' Well, you know what he meant…

JOHN INVERDALE

Grand National Day

The Radio Broadcaster of the Year for 1997, John Inverdale presented Sports Report *for seven years before moving on to host a daily* Drivetime *show and various major sporting occasions for Radio Five Live. He is a stalwart of Esher RUFC, and an enthusiastic but so far unfortunate National Hunt owner.*

National Hunt racing has a definable image. Barbours and green wellies in the members enclosure. Discarded *Sporting Lifes* and betting slips in the cheap seats. Not many sports attract such a cosmopolitan following from the Lord of the Manor to the man who cleans his Roller. And then there's Aintree – a world apart from any other steeplechasing venue. And there's the National – a race apart, with perhaps the richest history of any single sporting event in the calendar.

My Mum was a big fan of Gregory Peck. Like the rest of Britain in that spring of 1968, she sat down with her morning paper to pick the winner of the National, and lo and behold, there was this horse called Different Class. Trained by Peter Cazalet, ridden by David Mould and owned by Gregory Peck. 'I'm going to back that,' she announced to no one in particular. Somewhat against my better instinct we all sat down in front of the telly ... Different Class came third behind Red Alligator ... my Mum won 4 bob, and it seemed like such an amazing event, I asked if we could all go to it one day.

Twenty years later, I went to Aintree for the first time courtesy of *Sports Report*. The seasons dribbled by, and it became a benchmark for the end of a long hard season. As you got on the train to Lime Street, the light at the end of the tunnel was only five weeks away, when after 40-odd Saturdays in a row we'd meet at Wembley for the Cup Final and play that tune for the last time before the summer recess.

What sets Aintree apart is its clientele. By and large there aren't too many scousers in the Members' at Cheltenham. As you drive to the course on the morning of the greatest horse race in the world, see the ferries drifting across to Birkenhead, see the Liver building and dream of Nerys Hughes, find yourself humming 'Strawberry Fields' with a vision of Emlyn Hughes in your minds' eye, those 30 fences seem to embody the life and soul of a city. The year Rhyme 'n Reason won, a guy with a beard and a very big grin opened a suitcase on the train back from the course. 'Ere mate ... look at that,' he said to me. 'There's ten grand in there,' and indeed there was. The rain can be lashing down, the temperatures barely above freezing, but twenty thousand women from all across Merseyside will still be wearing mini-skirts that leave little to the imagination. Real people – not your Royal Ascot lot.

So Aintree is different, and because of that, and because the first winner was called Lottery, and because of Devon Loch, and Red Rum, and Bob Champion, and every other legendary tale etched into the sporting history books, when you pitch up at Aintree, by and large you think nothing can happen that will remotely take you by surprise.

That day in 1993 dawned bright as I recall. The age-old tradition of all those working on the programme was to set the alarm early, and head off to the course to watch the runners familiarise themselves with the course. 'Isn't that West Tip?' the producer would ask, looking at one of the police horses.

Four bacon butties later, as 10 o'clock struck, and the programme was just two hours away, we had what nominally passed as a production meeting, and finished it by saying that we'd do it like we'd always done it, and the culmination of the day would be the ceremonial presentation of Peter Bromley's racecard, with all his notes and colours, to the winning jockey, which the victorious rider would then frame and hang in his loo. It was like any other National morning. Walking round the weighing room, a hundred taut faces, one or two jockeys still on the look out for a spare ride should misfortune befall one of their colleagues. Everybody had a tip. 'Don't be daft ... he won't stay.' Reg Smith, the official Grand National historian, was reminiscing about days gone by, telling tales of Tommy Stack and 'Rummy', and at around half past eleven three of us walked the latter part of the course, from the Chair home, looking at empty grandstands but imagining the scene four hours later when, in typical National style, one of the runners would lead at the elbow, *à la* Crisp, only to be ensnared in the dying strides. There's something magical about major sporting arenas before the madding crowd arrives. Aintree was no different that day. At five past twelve I met up with our roving engineer, grabbed a microphone, and scribbled a few notes on my racecard. Lights. Camera. Action.

From Argentina to Australia, the world must have watched in disbelief as the remarkable events unfolded that day. Close your eyes and you can see those pictures of people sitting on the fences, of horses getting caught up in the starting tape, of the starter Keith Brown being pilloried as the man who made a laughing stock of the nation's sporting heritage.

At what point it dawned on us that the whole thing was degenerating into a complete shambles I don't remember. The first reports that animal rights demonstrators were seeking to disrupt the race seemed fanciful and exaggerated. Pat Thornton, the programme producer, despatched Mark Saggers, one of our reporters, down to the start, just in case.

The half hour that followed was testimony to radio's ability to respond to a breaking news story like no other medium. Trainers broke down in tears, jockeys dismounted and professed themselves speechless. Silence on radio can sometimes convey so much. As I waited to interview the winning connections by the unsaddling enclosure, officials scurried hither and thither. What on earth was going on? Nobody knew.

And meanwhile the race went on, minus half the field. The commentators, Tony O'Hehir, John Penney, Lee McKenzie and Peter Bromley, carried on regardless, prefacing every sentence with the words 'is this the National or isn't it?

And Esha Ness came storming home, and John White went a grief-stricken shade of ashen grey when he realised that the greatest moment in a jockey's life was to be denied him through such an extraordinary combination of circumstances, incompetence and sheer bloody-minded ignorance.

You're supposed to be reasoned and impartial when presenting radio programmes. At least that's what the manuals say. But it was impossible, surrounded by so many people for whom a year's preparations had gone up in smoke, not to feel consumed with anger and frustration on their behalf. No major sporting event – arguably the biggest single annual sporting event in the country – should be allowed to degenerate into such farce.

It all added to the mythology of the Grand National, of course. In a funny sort of way, it was a privilege to have been there. Boy did we have some stories to tell on the way home. *Sports Report* had shown itself to be editorially as sharp as a knife. The technical boys had done a fantastic job, getting cables to the most inaccessible parts of the course, and such a fine team effort deservedly got its just desserts with a prestigious Sony Award – a radio Oscar. I remember Pat saying, as the train pulled into Euston, 'Just think, you'll be able to say you were there on the only time the Grand National didn't take place.'

Fast forward four years. Ian Payne was *Sports Report*'s presenter by now. I'd thought about going up to Liverpool for pleasure as Charlie Brooks, Radio 5 Live's racing expert, a leading trainer and a great personal friend, had a very real chance of winning the race with the grey horse Sunybay. The prospect of a considerable party on that Saturday night was a major lure. We'd sat in a pub at Cheltenham three weeks before, and Charlie had whispered, not because he didn't want anybody to hear but because he felt he might be tempting the fates, 'He's got the most fantastic chance you know.' Then we spoke on the morning of the race. 'Ground's a bit quick, but you never know.' Trainer-speak for 'we're very confident'.

That afternoon, my rugby club won promotion to National Division Four, the culmination of a five-year plan to become one of the country's top 60 clubs. I was sitting in the stand at Esher when race-time came, and rushed off to the television in the bar. Chaos. No TV coverage. The course evacuated. In the run-up to the election campaign, the IRA had decided to target the one sporting event the whole of Ireland stops for.

For the first time in many, many years, *Sports Report* didn't come from Aintree. All the equipment was there, but, like the Marie Celeste, the course was like a ghost-ship. Only one man remained, Phil Sharp, Charlie's head lad who stayed behind in the stables to look after the runners. With 40 horses in his care, he didn't have time to say 'And the headlines tonight'…

The bulldog spirit was much in evidence. Terrorists were not going to sabotage the National. The show would go on, because it had to go on. If Aintree gave in, what would the next target be? On Saturday night, jockeys partied the night away at Liverpool hotels, still dressed in their silks, their ordinary clothes left hanging forlorn in the weighing room at the course. The Aintree executive pondered the options. On Sunday, they made their decision.

And so it was that the National was run on the Monday, and I ended up presenting a special edition of *Sports Report*. And believe me, it was very special. An odd eerie chill hung over the whole city. The train up to Aintree had been packed with journalists and film crews. It was almost as though we were all there as voyeurs, brought off the bench as second- half substitutes to gawk at a sporting freakshow. It was odd travelling to the course on a Monday, and the cordon of police that greeted you hundreds of yards from the course entrance was just the start. You needed a hundred identity passes and a letter from the Queen to get past the first checkpoint. And rightly so. There could be no repeat performance.

We planned the programme as much as we could. It was anybody's guess how many people would turn up. A well-known commentator (no names ...) had been trying on a very expensive coat at one of the course shops when the order to evacuate had been made. His conscience was pricking him ... should he take it back? (To this day, I don't know if he did.)

We had a rough idea about who we were going to talk to. Charlie was very bullish that the race should go on ... less bullish about Sunybay's chances. With every rain-free hour, the ground firmed up, and his prospects diminished. This was an extraordinary day in many ways – a one-race day, the Grand National and er ... that's it. Eight minutes. But as five o'clock neared, and instead of the *Sports Report* signature tune Peter Bromley prepared to say 'and they're under orders and they're off,' the thousands began to arrive. Prime Minister John Major had only a month left at Number 10, but when his helicopter landed and he walked into the parade ring to a rapturous reception, you knew this was something special. Not too many Tory MPs were returned on Merseyside, but that cheer was a symbolic gesture of defiance against the forces of evil. In the end between 25,000 and 30,000 people were there to witness Lord Gyllene's victory. More than 10,000 more were outside – they'd left work or home too late, and the security checks were too vigilant to allow a mass rush for the stands in the minutes before the off.

If 'How do you feel?' is the one question an interviewer is never supposed to ask, there was only one question to be asked of everyone involved in what turned out to be a relatively uneventful race: 'how did it feel?'

Was this the real deal, or just a run-of-the-mill 4-mile steeplechase masquerading as the world's greatest horse race? And they all said the same. The National is the National, even if it's run at 4.30 on a Thursday morning in August. Winning jockey Tony Dobbin said it was the pinnacle of his riding career, and the reception he received *en route* to the unsaddling enclosure would not have shamed Red Rum if he'd won the race a fourth time.

Sunybay came second. After challenging for 28 fences, there wasn't enough gas left in the tank as the home turn beckoned. 'Make no mistake,' said Charlie. 'This was a truly great sporting occasion. I'm so proud to have been part of it. Mind you, if only the winner had run out at the last...'

Whoever said sport and politics didn't mix was either absurdly naive or just plain dumb. The National that day was an occasion when the two collided head on. Our coverage demanded a measure of sensitivity, as well as tub-thumping. It was more than just a horse race, it was a major news story being beamed around the world. The political world that day focused on Bechers, The Chair and Valentines. It was one of those days when you're not just privileged to be present at an historic moment, but proud to be part of a team, led by producer Gill Pulsford and editor Rob Hastie, with the sureness of touch to get the balance just right.

Grand National Saturday is, year in year out, the most complex single operation mounted by the Radio Sport department. It seems that, each and every year, the race provides a story of human or equine endeavour to amaze, thrill, sadden and inspire. From Feydeau farce in 1993 to political pawn in 1997, it holds a unique place in the British sporting calendar, and *Sports Report* has been there since Sheila's Cottage won in 1948. Twenty-one years into the programme's history... Twenty-nine years ago, Highland Wedding won the race for trainer Toby Balding. I mention that because it's the only time I've backed the winner.

CHRISTOPHER MARTIN-JENKINS

Cricket in the 1970s: Lillee and Thomson

Formerly BBC Cricket Correspondent and now the respected correspondent of the Daily Telegraph, *Christopher Martin-Jenkins was himself a talented batsman, while his son Robin is a promising Sussex all-rounder. Chris is the current Sports Reporter of the Year.*

It was chance that brought together the greatest fast-bowling partnership of my years as a privileged cricket correspondent. Dennis Lillee was dark, hard, fit, cunning and malevolent, with a long and magnificent run-up; and his final leap into delivery had all the vigour of an Alpine ski-jumper. Jeff Thomson was casual, amiable and unconventional, more interested in the beach and his surfboard during his Sydney youth than in the stern disciplines of cricket. But he was as strong as a well-muscled ox and with a full swing of a strong right arm he could propel a cricket ball faster than the stone with which David slew Goliath from his sling.

Together they formed, with ideal back-up from Max Walker (a big man who, as the Aussies say, could hoop it around at will), the most formidable pair of fast bowlers to have worked in unison during the last quarter of the 20th century. In their wake, the West Indies produced great pairs of their own, and other pairs in support so that the problem for the batsman was no longer mainly against the new ball; rather against a remorseless quartet operating at their own chosen pace all day long. It altered the whole approach to Test cricket and made the West Indies, with great batsmen to finish the job, virtually unbeatable for a lengthy period. But until Thomson injured his shoulder and lost consistency, Lillee and Thommo were the stuff of batsmen's nightmares.

Lillee had been the outstanding fast bowler of the England versus Australia series of 1972 and the quickest on either side since Frank Tyson, with Brian Statham's unremitting assistance, had helped England to regain the Ashes in 1954–55. But his back failed him in the West Indies a few months later and there was no guarantee at all that he would be fit to play against Mike Denness's England touring team in 1974–75.

Thommo was unknown outside Australia when that tour began and no more than one of several promising young bowlers as far as all but a very few Australians were concerned. He had caught the eye in six Sheffield Shield cricket games for New South Wales sufficiently to be selected for Australia, in the injured Lillee's absence, against Pakistan in 1972–73. He took no wickets for 110, as it later transpired with a broken bone in his foot.

When an experienced England side arrived in Australia in October 1974, there seemed nothing for them to be unduly worried about. Of Thomson they were in blithe ignorance and there was still a possibility that Lillee might not win his fight to recover from a stress fracture. If he did, the speculation was that he could not be the same tearaway. Having first established himself with his amazing analysis of 8 for 29 against the Rest of the World three years earlier at Perth and quickly became the spearhead of his country's attack, his long battle for fitness was the talk of the Australian press.

Indeed John Inverarity, his State captain, took the then unusual course of arranging special new conferences on condition that the pride of Western Australia was not bothered at home. He had played no serious cricket since breaking down some 18 months before and in the winter before the Ashes series he had spent three nights a week on a training programme which combined four mile runs, isometric exercises and weight-lifting. With fateful timing his first comeback match for Western Australia against South Australia coincided with the arrival in Adelaide of the MCC team for their early-tour muscle stretching and net practice.

Lillee duly produced a five wicket analysis, bowling to a new formula, not flat out all the time but, like Ray Lindwall, concentrating on fast-medium swing with the occasional quick one, as the Aussies say 'to keep the batsman honest'. He was to keep plenty of hapless Poms honest over the next few months as the confidence in his physical recovery grew.

The unfortunate Denness and his team had no foreknowledge that there would be someone even quicker at the other end. Geoff Boycott had refused to tour, for reasons never entirely explained but thought to have been a mixture of his opposition to Denness's elevation to the captaincy and his own frustration about failures against modest little Indian medium-pacers, but England still had two opening batsmen of high class in John Edrich and Dennis Amiss, both of whom would join the immortals by scoring more than a hundred first-class hundreds. Oddly, Edrich did not open during this series, batting instead at three or four.

I shall never forget Amiss's first meeting with Thomson, although it was actually Lillee who was to plague him for the rest of his career whenever the baggy green caps were around. Thomson had moved to Queensland from New South Wales and I was by no means the only one on or off the field seeing him for the first time when England played their last State match before the first Test on the same ground: the Gabba at Brisbane.

Thommo's run was not especially long, stylish or quirky – as straightforward as the man himself in fact – but the final sweep of the arm came from somewhere near his right ankle as he took aim with one eye over his left shoulder and pivoted from this perfect sideways-on position from a braced front leg. It was like a boxer's haymaker punch or the golf swing of Tiger Woods: compacted power released with maximum efficiency.

That first ball rose sharply from a length and zipped back

into a startled Amiss's solar plexus. It was an instant warning and it did not go unnoticed. Thomson got Amiss out in both innings and although his figures were not particularly remarkable, his raw pace was. He was picked for the first Test on the strength of one for 22 in the first innings and one for 29 in the second. The selectors had seen all they wanted to see, perhaps, when Amiss recoiled instinctively at that first ball.

Ten days later Thomson's Test career was properly launched. He took the first three England wickets in the game after Bob Willis had warned his colleagues of what might be to come by getting help from an underprepared pitch and finishing his first Ashes match with nine for 105. Lillee took four wickets and another four at his native Perth as he began to trust his back and to marry a genuine mastery of swing and seam to his original pace. Thomson took seven and Australia won again.

So it went on. There were eight more scalps for the laconic Thommo in the excitingly drawn third Test but on a hard green pitch at Sydney in the new year it was no contest. By the time that England, for this one match under the command of the unflinching John Edrich, had lost the match by 171 runs and the Ashes too, Lillee and Thommo were Australian folk heroes. This was the game in which Keith Fletcher was very nearly caught at cover by Ross Edwards from a deflected top edge onto his forehead. Never has a cricket ball flown further off a man's head; perhaps not even a football. When Fletcher was asked for his autograph at Hobart airport the following day, David Lloyd looked over his shoulder and said, 'What are you signing, Keith, Nat Lofthouse?'

As a hunting pair, they were equally devastating in only one more series, against the West Indies the following year, but Lillee, the supreme athlete and craftsman combined, went on to take 355 wickets in 70 Tests before using his considerable intelligence and articulacy to become an exceptional coach. Thommo, liked by everyone once the day's play was over, took 200 wickets in 51 games. They are a legend still.

ALAN GREEN

Life as a Commentator

*One of Radio Sport's most distinctive voices,
Alan Green is an outspoken presence among the
football commentators, and also reports on golf
and rowing. Voted No. 1 Sports Broadcaster
for 1997, Alan presents his own* Sports Talk
discussion programme.

Talk to *any* commentator currently working in BBC Radio
Sport and they'll tell you how very different the working
environment is now compared with ten, never mind fifty years
ago. Certainly, in terms of football, the demands imposed seem
infinitely greater. The late Peter Jones, once the senior football
commentator, would have been required to share a second-half
commentary on a Saturday afternoon, as well as the odd game
on a Tuesday or Wednesday evening. Today, even those fresh
into the field are expected to cope with three games a week. It's
unusual for me not to manage over one hundred football
commentaries each season and, in a World Cup or European
Championship year, many more than that.

Yet, before I sat down to write this, I was moved to read
a chapter, entitled 'The Commentator', from the first book
on *Sports Report*, written by the very great Raymond
Glendenning. I was surprised at how much then is relevant to
life as I know it now. There was the natural, but not always
justified, assumption that the commentator gets 'the best view
of the game'. There was the criticism that the commentator

gets too excited and that he or she is biased, bluntly ignoring the fact that 'nine times out of ten' the listeners 'are not impartial themselves'. Perhaps, nothing of significance really changes.

Frequently, I do have the best seat in the house. I remember sitting in the Rose Bowl in Pasadena, before the 1994 World Cup Final between Brazil and Italy, thinking that if anyone, beforehand, had offered me a choice of seats, I would have chosen this one. It had the perfect elevation for commentary, not so low that you lose perspective, not so high that you feel you're watching 'subbutteo'. It was directly positioned over the half-way line and no more than ten yards behind a beautifully decorated podium on which stood the World Cup trophy itself. I felt as if I could reach out and touch it, just as easily as Dunga did once Brazil had won that dreadfully disappointing game on penalties.

But that commentary position had a geographic penalty all of its own. The blistering Californian sun shone directly down on our heads. You see, the Rose Bowl offers no cover. It hardly ever experiences rain. Why would you need a roof? So, there were two serious consequences for those charged with describing the games there. You needed protection from the sun and there had to be some means of preventing the glare destroying any opportunity of watching the television monitors provided at each position. (No commentator relies exclusively on television pictures to 'tell the tale' but, when a monitor is available, rarely the case in radio, it does help as 'back-up'.)

The American organisers, finally recognising 'problem two', provided large cardboard boxes to help cover the TV screens. I solved 'problem one' by wearing the box on my head! It wasn't, I grant you, the most fashion-conscious solution but I would argue it was far less silly to look at than John Motson's lurid green sombrero!

Wembley Stadium offers one of the very best positions from which to view a game. You would expect it to, and I hope that, when the grand old lady is completely re-constructed over the next couple of years, suitable attention is paid to the commentators' vantage points. There is ONE deficiency, though, and I'll be very pleased to see it disappear!

Some time ago, the 'BBC radio box' was moved higher and further forward to its present 'eagle's eyrie' of a position, slung beneath the roof. We actually have to walk along a metal gangway through girders to reach it. Once there, the view is magnificently uninterrupted. If a commentator gets it 'wrong' at Wembley, he usually only has himself to blame. But you can't physically see the Royal Box. To describe the presentation of a trophy, the commentator must rely on a television monitor.

Imagine, then, my predicament at the climax to the 1993 League Cup Final when Arsenal had beaten Sheffield Wednesday. Remember those joyous Gunners' celebrations during which the captain, Tony Adams, 'dropped' Steve Morrow, breaking the Ulsterman's shoulder? Watching on, you couldn't tell the extent of the injury but Morrow wasn't moving, the stretcher was on the pitch and, clearly, the presentation ceremony had to be delayed.

ITV was covering the game and providing our pictures in the commentary box. The director must have decided that the call of commercials was too strong to resist and took a 'break' in the transmission from Wembley to show ads. What I didn't know then but soon did, to my complete horror, was that he'd also decided to let the presentation happen during the commercial break and then 'play it in' later as if it was live even though it was actually on video. I only grasped what was going on when Adams shrugged his shoulders, leaving Morrow with his damaged one, and led the Arsenal players up the steps to the Royal Box and out of my sight! When the monitor should have been showing me the trophy being lifted, I was really watching an ad for washing-up liquid! In commentary parlance, I 'busked' the whole ceremony because I didn't see a thing. I've never quite forgiven ITV.

It must be a coincidence, surely, but much the worst commentary 'positions' that I've experienced have been in the company of my dear friend, the former England captain, Jimmy Armfield. He won't forget, as I won't, the garden shed that was hung on top of scaffolding as we watched Hartlepool United famously beat Crystal Palace in the FA Cup 3rd round. The contraption was mere inches from the touchline. I remember thinking I could tap the linesman on the shoulder and tell him directly that we disagreed with his offside decision.

It was similarly cold in Innsbruck watching Liverpool play in a European tie but we hardly noticed. We were commentating from a hut (which also housed the public address system!) perched on top of a hamburger stall alongside a corner flag! The resultant heat was welcome, the stench less so.

Most memorable of all, though, was a game we did together in Moscow in 1992. Manchester United were playing in the UEFA Cup against Torpedo. The Russian capital that September was a dark, cold, forbidding place to visit, but we'd been to the ramshackle stadium the day before the match and consoled ourselves in the knowledge, we thought, that we'd be ensconced in one of the few tiny enclosed boxes at the back of the main stand.

It was an awful afternoon, pitch dark at 3pm, torrential rain. Jimmy and I arrived quite late at the ground because the media bus had been diverted to collect one of the tour guide's relatives! I was due 'on air' very shortly so I ran into the stadium and up the steps towards my perceived position. I heard a scream. It was the outside broadcast producer who'd gone along earlier. He stood on the surrounding running track looking like a drowned rat. 'Don't blame me,' he pleaded, 'it's not my fault. Just follow me.'

So close to a broadcast, I wasn't in a position to argue. I followed him towards one end of the ground. Across the track, opposite a corner flag, stood a single-decker bus. He ushered me on board. "This," he explained, "is where they've put the lines!" I had two options. I could burst into tears and throw a prima-donna tantrum OR I could laugh and get on with it. I chose the latter.

The game finished 0–0, went into extra-time, and United lost on penalties. The whole commentary was conducted with me leaning out of one of those narrow slotted bus windows. I kept asking Jimmy to have his pensioner's bus pass available in case the conductor came along. The comedy, like the afternoon, was very black. The highlight for me was the time an elderly man came along and tried to wipe the windows with a dirty rag. All he did was smear them and make matters worse. To this day, people mention that bus to me but few remember the result of the game. An artist was even given to sketching the scene as he imagined it from our commentary. It hangs on a wall in my house.

Someone once called me the Victor Meldrew of football commentary. It wasn't meant as a criticism. He enjoyed the way I moaned if I was wet or cold or miserable. He understood that if I didn't tell you when I wasn't enjoying a game or a situation you might not trust me if I say what a wonderful match this is or what a great time I'm having. I suppose, if you were determined, you could 'cheat' on radio. After all, listening to the radio commentator might be the only way you can 'see' the event. But, what would be the point of misleading you?

I've known commentators who 'invent' pictures to bring to the listeners. 'I can see a tall man, just three rows in front of me, wearing a blue and white striped top hat. Heaven knows where he bought it!' I certainly couldn't tell you because the man in the top hat didn't exist. Why invent pictures when they are all around you anyway? If you go to games you'll know yourself. What of those people who never seem to know the kick-off time and *always* arrive late? They fumble their way to the seat in front of you obscuring your view of that free-kick that whizzed by the far post. Just as bad, are those who leave <u>early</u> either before half-time or the final whistle, no matter the state of the game, anxious to buy their Bovril or beat the traffic. Do they care whether or not they're bothering you? Get the picture? It's one I try to bring to those listening.

A commentator on radio must deliver the 'whole picture', not merely describing the game itself but what's happening around and because of it. After all, that's what you'd get if you were able to attend yourself. It's my job to 'take you there'.

I think complete honesty is essential. You watch as many bad games as good ones. I believe it's vital to reflect accurately what you're seeing. It shouldn't be the job of a commentator to act as a salesman for the sport. If it doesn't 'sell' itself through the quality of the spectacle it offers then that's the sport's problem not the commentator's. Of course, he must entertain or else he will lose his audience. That can be difficult if you're watching drivel.

Strangely, I always feel I've taken something valuable from a game even if it wasn't good to watch. It's mostly because I love football (how else could I bear watching so much of it?) but also because I love broadcasting. As a highly emotional Irishman, I like to wallow in the highs and lows of the events I'm privileged to see. I allow my broadcasting to ride the same rollercoaster every sporting spectator will have experienced.

The lows have sometimes been very difficult to cope with. I was the commentator describing the opening minutes of the FA Cup semi-final in 1989 between Liverpool and Nottingham Forest before it became no longer a football match but the Hillsborough tragedy. As Peter Jones and myself struggled to bring you the horrors of that afternoon, I remember a fleeting but important thought going through my mind about the problems facing Mike Ingham and Bryon Butler who had to continue relaying news of the other semi at Villa Park whilst knowing of its insignificance in relation to events unfolding in Sheffield. Nine years on, Hillsborough still affects me.

I laugh a lot watching football. I also cry. On the last day of the 1986–87 season, the Division 1 Championship already decided in favour of Everton, Peter Jones and I were surprisingly dispatched to Turf Moor. It seemed an odd decision to make regarding the final league commentary of the season. Burnley, one of the founder members of the Football League, were then in the old Division lV and playing Leyton Orient in a game that would help decide whether they'd be relegated to non-league football. The ground was full. Burnley had to win but even then had to rely on favourable results elsewhere. It was one of the most emotional games I've ever experienced. Burnley survived. People openly cried tears of relief as well as joy. Both commentators unashamedly joined in. It was a memorable day and the right commentary to do.

With very few exceptions, I never listen to anything I've done. It'll surprise many who assume broadcasters are, of necessity, vain, but I can't stand the sound of my own voice. It's one of the benefits of being 'live' ... it's happened ... it's gone ... you can't affect it ... why listen to it?

One exception is the commentary from England's World Cup semi-final meeting with Germany in Turin, 1990. When Lineker equalised. I had no idea, as few of us 'on the road' in Italy had, about the impact the tournament was making back in Britain. We only knew when we returned.

The night of the German game, the Rolling Stones held a concert at Wembley. During one of the numbers, a huge roar broke out around the stadium. Mick Jagger couldn't understand and stopped singing. He looked off-stage. 'What's going on?' 'Lineker's equalised,' he was told. People had gone to Wembley to watch one of the great rock bands but many were carrying transistor radios to follow the game. My commentary had stopped a Rolling Stones concert! 'Lineker with a great chance ... and it's there ... Gary Lineker has done it for England!' Inane, I know, but a great memory. I can stand listening to that.

Perhaps it's because I watch so much football, but my best memories in commentary from recent years are from my fleeting appearances in other sports. I can't believe how lucky I was to be asked, more than ten years ago, to work on golf. Open championships, Ryder Cups, are such wonderful events. Some accuse the BBC Radio team of being overly patriotic on such occasions. Nonsense, I say. Of course there is a natural inclination to want a British golfer or Europe to win. Similarly, I always want an English club to win in Europe or England to win an international. But it *never* affects my objective view of what I'm describing. A commentator must *always* appreciate what he's watching, whoever's doing well, whoever's winning.

When you take into account the expansion of the football season, almost a year-round sport now, and throw in the odd golf tournament, there's isn't much time left for anything else. I was initially dubious when the Head of Sport, Bob Shennan, asked me if I'd commentate on rowing at the Atlanta Olympics. What did I know about rowing? Nothing. I can't even swim. But the challenge enticed me, particularly once I'd met some of the people in the sport. I can't honestly say I like everyone in football. I don't. But there hasn't been anyone I've met in rowing that I didn't immediately warm to.

I worked hard at getting to know the sport as well as its people. I think they appreciated my honesty ('I don't know rowing. Please help.') By the time Georgia was no longer on my mind but reality, I was pretty much prepared.

The Olympic Regatta at Lake Lanier was one of the best experiences of my life. I can't tell you how much I enjoyed it. I felt wholly involved with a sport that is, arguably, the most demandingly athletic of them all and, most certainly, is amongst the most honest. For me, too, the event had the most appropriate climax.

A primary reason why I had been asked to commentate on the sport was that we anticipated a British gold medal for Steven Redgrave and Matthew Pinsent in the Coxless Pairs event. Mentally, I'd been gearing myself up to describing this key moment. Strangely, subconsciously, I must have been thinking about it for ten months.

The night before the final, I lay awake in my motel bedroom thinking about the race. I'll bet Steve and Matt slept much better than I did! At 3am I gave up and switched on the television to discover that there'd been a bombing in Centennial Park in Atlanta, some 60 miles away. For a while, the future of the whole Olympics appeared in doubt. I was transfixed ... and concerned.

Around 6am the phone rang. It was Bob Shennan explaining that he and Jenny Abramsky, then Controller of BBC 5 Live, couldn't get out to Lake Lanier as they'd intended. They couldn't even get out of their Atlanta hotel! He wished me well for the commentary. "Oh ... one thing, Greenie ... make sure it's Gold! We could do with it.' (Britain had yet to win a gold in that Olympics – as it transpired, this was to be the only one.)

The race went like a dream. The Australians challenged but knew that, on this day, they wouldn't be even nearly good enough. Redgrave and Pinsent were magnificent. I'm pleased and relieved to say the commentary wasn't that bad either. I felt in tandem with their performance. It was as if I, too, had trained for four years for this moment. Had got up at five in the morning and got the boat out onto the River Thames at Henley, no matter the winter weather. I hadn't, of course, but emotionally they'd allow me to share, however briefly, in their fantastic triumph. That's the ultimate privilege allowed to a sports commentator. It's why I wouldn't swap my job for anyone else's.

CHRISTOPHER INGLEBY

A Listener's View

*Christopher Ingleby of Bradford describes
himself as 'a long-time fan of the Five o'clock
Show'. He wrote in to the programme to describe
his experiences as a listener.*

I am 48 now, and when I was a youngster my Dad used to take
me every other week to watch the old Bradford Park Avenue
Football Club, in what was up to 1958 the old Third Division
(North) and afterwards Division Four. They never aspired to
any greater heights than that, sad to say – at least not in the time
that I watched them.

   We didn't own a television set in the late 50s (not many
around us did) so we used to chase out of the ground minutes
before the final whistle to be sure of getting on one of the Soccer
Special buses away from the ground which in turn would get us
home for around 4.55pm – just time to 'warm up' the old valve
wireless in order to hear Eamonn Andrews announce the Five
o'clock Headlines. By this time Dad would have delved into the
sideboard drawer for his crumpled Vernons copy-coupon in
time religiously to follow the voice of John Webster as he read
out the day's results – his tone and inflexion of speech as he read
each result indicating a Home Win, Away Win or magical
Draw! (Just draws in those days – no 'no-score' or 'score' draws
as now.) John's style of reading was similar to that of the late
Len Marten on *Grandstand* and James Alexander Gordon on
present-day *Sports Report*.

At the enquiring age of ten or eleven, I often wondered as I sat munching my hurriedly-prepared toasted teacake while listening to the match reports from around the country, why it was always stories from places such as Burnley, Wolverhampton, Arsenal and Everton – never Hartlepool, Bury, Doncaster or Accrington Stanley, and certainly never Bradford PA! However, all that changed in 1967, when Bradford were drawn at home to Fulham in the third round of the FA Cup – Fulham were in the old First Division then of course! We all queued for tickets and were lucky to get two in the old stand to see Johnny Haynes (by then approaching the end of his career), 1966 World Cup hero George Cohen, and perhaps a glimpse of Tommy ('You Lucky People!') Trinder as he might be finding his way through the low County Cricket Stand which was positioned back-to-back with the football stand in the shared Park Avenue complex.

Well, no sign of Tommy (probably in pantomime somewhere, as it was January). What we, and the rest of the 14,000-plus crowd, did witness was a victory (though not an emphatic one) by the Cottagers – 3 goals to 1. Spells of the old magic from Haynes and a fairly quiet afternoon for Peter Mellor in the Fulham goal, who was beaten just the once by Bradford's inside-forward, Phil Robinson. Then came the usual race home after the game for *Sports Report*, which, because it was Cup third round day and Bradford were at home to a First Division side, carried a live report on the game. The line was a bit crackly – it really did sound to be coming via cocoa tins and elastic – but it didn't matter a jot to me and my Dad. I sat spellbound listening to Bradford's somewhat sorry Cup exit relayed, incident by incident, courtesy of the voice at the end of the wire. I remember thinking to myself 'What a marvellous thing this wireless is – to think he's talking to us from just down the road!'

I've remained an avid listener to BBC Radio Sport throughout the thirty-five years or so since my Dad and I used to tune in faithfully to *Sports Report*, and, if we were not attending a match ourselves that week, 'Association Football' commentary at 3.45pm on the Saturday afternoon – I can just about recall the fast voice of Raymond Glendenning. I still derive immense pleasure from listening to the very interesting commentators and reporters behind the mikes who bring all the very best sporting action to the Five Live listener, and I would like to end by sending my very best wishes to all connected with *Sports Report*.

JOHN RAWLING

On Track

*John Rawling, the BBC's Athletics
Correspondent and boxing commentator, also
reports on football and is a former Sports
Broadcaster of the year. One of several sporting
graduates from BBC Radio Leicester, John is a
collector of classic cars, and a man about town.*

In 1991, at the World Athletics Championships in Tokyo, four
British men created history. Roger Black, John Regis, Derek
Redmond and Kriss Akabusi brought Britain its first 400 metre
relay gold medal in a World Championship, beating the
favourites, the USA, in a stunning conclusion to the week's events.

The sight of Akabusi, the 400 metre hurdler, in pursuit of the
world champion Antonio Pettigrew on the final leg created one
of those indelible sporting memories for anyone who witnessed
it. Taking over the baton a metre or so behind, Akabusi bided
his time. Then, almost unbelievably, in the final straight sheer
force of will seemed to propel him past Pettigrew to cross the
line ahead.

Commentating at the time with Mike Whittingham, who
coached three members of the team, I remember it was hard to
maintain any semblance of perspective. Hell, who cared, it was
a British win and let's face it there are not too many of them: it
was the right moment to go ballistic.

A friend confided afterwards that he had been driving down
Brighton sea front at the time in a car filled with his young and

excitable family. Rather than collide with oncoming traffic as he pounded the steering wheel with all around him shrieking and shouting during Akabusi's epic glory dash, or take an unscheduled left turn on to the shingle, he pulled over. 'Anyone who doubts if athletics works on the radio needs to take a listen to that,' he said.

At the same Championships, Mike Powell and the great Carl Lewis locked horns in the long jump, with Powell ultimately almost leaping out of the pit not only to take the gold but also to break Bob Beamon's world record which had stood since the Mexico Olympics of 1968. Bob Phillips, that doyen of the statistic and a familiar voice to listeners, had seen Beamon destroy Ralph Boston, Lynn Davies and the rest in Mexico. His excitement and sense of wonder was genuine in Tokyo as he told his audience: 'I never believed that I would see the day when Beamon was bettered.'

But athletics never ceases in its capacity to surprise and amaze. Nor does it take second best to any sport in its ability to generate what might be termed the 'feelgood factor'. As Powell and Lewis embarked on their battle, a blind international golfer was listening somewhere on a train heading out of London. He told me later: 'I was sitting in a crowded railway carriage. I'd had a few beers and had my radio headset on. The world record went, and I just started shouting. People must have thought that I was crazy, and the guard had to come and tell me to shut up.' Big Dave had been totally blind since the age of eight. He never saw Powell, but the radio almost convinced him that he had.

BBC Radio's reputation as an athletics broadcaster has grown to the point where listeners have long since gained the Test Match Special habit: turn down the sound on the telly and take the commentary off the wireless. While other nations' radio stations report on the events, no other network builds programmes around the sport as does good old Auntie.

From Raymond Glendenning and Harold Abrahams to Rex Alston and Norman Cuddeford; then, in more recent years, with Alan Parry and Peter Matthews, Ian Darke, Bob Phillips,

Mike Whittingham and myself, athletics broadcasting has developed to become an integral part of BBC sporting output which hopefully commands the affection of those on the track as well as the listeners.

Dave Moorcroft, former 5,000 metres world record holder and now Chief Executive of the British Athletics Federation, has become familiar to television viewers and radio listeners for the calm authority of his commentaries. 'In many ways I prefer the radio work,' he says.

> Some sports struggle without pictures, but often athletics is more exciting on the radio. When you work in television, by the very nature of it you're governed by the pictures. But when I work in radio, I'm very conscious that the words I use create the pictures. As well as that, the medium gives you time to pursue arguments and to be more reflective in your approach than you can ever be in television. It gives you so much more flexibility.

The era of Moorcroft the athlete coincided with that of Alan Parry the commentator. 'I remember particularly a great commentary which Alan did in 1984 at the AAA Championships, when Peter Elliott beat Seb Coe in the 1500,' Moorcroft added, 'but I never really heard any of his commentaries on my races. Radio's all about being live, so the athletes rarely hear the commentaries on themselves.'

Parry's radio days spanned the glory years of Coe, Steve Ovett and Steve Cram, of Allan Wells and Daley Thompson. It all began for him back in 1974, with commentary on Brendan Foster's world 3,000 metres record at the newly opened Gateshead Stadium.

> I remember it was in the old days of Sport On Two. I'd been sent to cover Bren's race. All there was at the stadium was one stand, a load of cinder banks and a BBC commentary box for television. I literally had to climb on to the top of the box and commentate into a tape recorder. It was peeing it down as well. Then I clambered down to

Virginia Wade, triumphant against all odds at Wimbledon during Jubilee year, 1977.

Headingley 1981: Ian Botham hits another boundary off Geoff Lawson on his way to an undefeated 149.

'You cannot be serious…' John McEnroe engaged in light banter with the umpire at Wimbledon.

Dennis Lillee leaps into his delivery stride and sends another shell-shocked batsman on his way.

*Peter Taylor and Brian Clough guiding Nottingham Forest to success.
Clough's signature green jersey came later.*

Scotland's Sandy Lyle winning the Open at Royal St George's, Sandwich, in 1985.

Nigel Mansell, Formula One World Champion at last after the 1992 Hungarian Grand Prix.

Hillsborough 1989: a poignant tribute to 96 Liverpool fans who lost their lives.

Nick Faldo, Britain's greatest-ever golfer with six majors and a record eleven Ryder Cup appearances.

The infamous 'Ball from Hell'. Ian Healy celebrates as Mike Gatting is bamboozled by Shane Warne at Old Trafford in 1993

'Tickets, please...' Alan Green and Jimmy Armfield on the buses in Moscow.

The end of the dream: Gazza weeps after the World Cup semi-final defeat by West Germany in 1990.

Three down, four to go. Frankie Dettori is airborne after winning the 1996 Queen Elizabeth Stakes on Mark of Esteem at Ascot.

South African President Nelson Mandela presents the 1995 Rugby World Cup trophy to victorious captain François Pienaar.

Matthew Pinsent and Steve Redgrave strike gold on Lake Lanier at the 1996 Olympic Games.

Manchester United celebrate victory over Chelsea in the 1997 Charity Shield – their 12th major trophy under Alex Ferguson.

Grand National day, 1997. Aintree race course is evacuated on police orders in response to a bomb threat.

send my recording back to London from the television outside broadcast van, and somehow it eventually got on air. And people say that it is a glamorous job!

Parry recalls fondly the Coe and Ovett years:

> It seemed that Seb and Steve were swapping world records every week at one time. By then, we'd persuaded the BBC that radio should be covering the major European meetings, so I was able to see many of their fantastic runs. In those days, Seb was very approachable and friendly and Steve was very much more aloof. Strange that it should have been Steve who finished up being such a good friend of mine when he joined me to commentate for ITV.

Watching Coe twice win the Olympic gold medal in the 1500, and seeing Ovett outfox Coe to win the 800 metres gold in Moscow, rank high in Parry's memories of that era of British middle-distance greatness. But it was the night when Steve Cram broke the world 1500 metres record in Nice in 1985 which he remembers with the biggest smile of all:

> Crammy was always such a great lad – terrific fun to be with. He beat Said Aouita in Nice, which was a fantastic achievement at the time. And of course he was taken off afterwards to doping control for his drugs test. Crammy being Crammy, he didn't take cups of water to give his urine sample, he was swigging back bottles of beer – on an empty stomach of course. So by the time we left the stadium for a night out, he was flying. I remember driving along the smart sea front in Nice, among all the millionaires, with Steve hanging out of the taxi window chanting Sunderland football songs and shouting to everybody that he'd just broken the world record. In the nightclub later, we got on to the champagne and Steve wound up on stage with the band playing bongo drums. What a night!

When Parry and his co-commentator, the estimable Peter Matthews, were lured into the television world to join ITV, it was Ian Darke, radio's boxing commentator, who took over Parry's microphone to follow the deeds of the world's athletes along with Bob Phillips. They witnessed a new era of British success, notably at the European Championships in Stuttgart in 1986, when Britain took nine gold medals. But all else pales into insignificance for Darke compared with the part he played in bringing to listeners news of one of the great sporting stories of the century as Ben Johnson tested positive for drugs at the Seoul Olympics in 1988. He recalls:

Johnson had just run the fastest 100 metres of all time, 9.78 seconds, beating Carl Lewis and Linford Christie. And we were just getting used to the idea that here was a phenomenal new star from Canada who was setting new standards that nobody else could touch. The news that he'd failed the test came in the middle of the night before the rest day they always have at the Olympics. Everybody had stayed up for a few drinks and a decent meal to relax and recharge the batteries. I'd gone to bed at the end of the evening and was fast asleep when the phone rang in my hotel bedroom. It was the Sports Editor, Mike Lewis. He just said: 'Darkie, wake up and wake up quickly. Don't say anything, just get a pencil and write this down and be prepared to broadcast in four minutes. I jotted down what he told me, put the 'phone down and 30 seconds later I was on air. It was the old five to ten sports desk in the evening – remember we were seven or eight hours ahead. The presenter said: 'First the sensational news from Seoul, where Ben Johnson has failed a drugs test, here's Ian Darke... Somehow, bleary eyed, I managed to scramble my way through my notes and do the report. After that the 'phone just didn't stop. It was the biggest sports story I have ever been involved in. And it tainted the whole sport, because whenever somebody performed well then, it became like a giant whodunnit. Are they on drugs? The 100 metres is always the Blue Riband event and for Johnson it was literally a case of from hero to zero.

Britain's Europa Cup triumph in 1989, watched for BBC Radio by Ian Darke and Dave Moorcroft, has been hailed as the beginning of the modern age of glory. New stars were emerging, and the brightest of them all was Linford Christie, the best sprinter ever to run for Britain. It was in Gateshead that Christie was asked to receive the trophy, as team captain. There had never been call for a captain before but, as team manager Les Jones said at the time: 'Somebody had to do it, so we asked Linford.' And Christie remained as figurehead for the next seven years. His relationship with the press was at best uneasy and at worst downright hostile. In turns aggressive, emotional, sensitive and headstrong, he was nevertheless fiercely committed to his sport and to his country. As Carl Lewis waned as the dominant figure in world sprinting, it was Christie who emerged as the number one.

With athletics firmly established on radio, and switched to the new Radio Five network, more athletics than ever before was broadcast from the Barcelona Olympics in 1992. And, with gold medals for Christie in the 100 metres and Sally Gunnell in the 400 metres hurdles, there was much to shout about.

For Christie, it was the fulfilment of a dream. After finishing fourth in the 100 metres the previous year at the World Championships in Japan, he had threatened to quit. But a year later his sprint for glory was magnificent at the age of 32. Gunnell, for her part, gave new purpose to the women's sport, and her smile was to prove as endearing to the nation as it was for those who commentated on her runs and interviewed her on a regular basis.

Colin Jackson's glory year was 1993. His run at the World Championships in Stuttgart in the 110 metres hurdles brought him the world record and, arguably, it was the high spot of the games for Britain as Tony Jarrett chased him home for the silver medal. Gunnell and Christie took gold once more and, for Gunnell, there was the added bonus of a world record. With the giant javelin thrower Steve Backley a perennial medal contender, Roger Black emerging from his injury problems to become Europe's number one 400 metres runner and Jonathan

Edwards breaking the world triple jump record at the World Championships in Gothenburg in 1995, British performers continued to create headlines.

The fabulous run of success had to end somewhere, and it did at the Atlanta Olympics. The Games were illuminated by stupendous performances, most notably from Michael Johnson and Donovan Bailey, but Britain returned without a gold. And there was much left to be desired off the track for the commentators. The triumph of Barcelona was emphasised by the organisational shambles of Atlanta. Chaotic transport services, a patently inadequate Olympic stadium and a Games which went some way towards surrendering Olympic ideals in exchange for commercial gain contrived together to make an unsatisfactory experience. Many of the broadcasters were glad to see the back of Georgia.

Coverage of the European Grand Prix athletics circuit has become a vital part of the summer's radio sport which athletics fans have come to expect. Zürich, Brussels and Oslo produce nights of great entertainment, but the process of reporting is not always easy. Slogging through the airport terminals of Europe can be a demanding task and arriving at a stadium to find that broadcasting facilities have not been installed is frustration defined. Cock-ups can happen anywhere, but Paris in 1995 was perhaps the *pièce de résistance*. No television monitor, no results monitor (at least for the first few events), and no broadcast line for the entire evening. So, Mike Whittingham and I were left to pass a telephone handset between us to provide commentary.

And try touring the world's stadia when your leg is in plaster because of a broken ankle, which was my lot in the summer of 1994. After falling at the World Championships in Helsinki, I was still on crutches by the time I arrived in Victoria for the Commonwealth Games in Canada later in the summer. To my horror, the commentary position was on a tower at the back of the stand, reached by trudging up 125 steps. Certainly, I would never have won a medal on the track, but if you could have put all the athletes on crutches by the end of the Games I could have been a contender.

To be a trackside reporter is no easy job. Being 6 feet 4 inches, as Andy Kay is, certainly helps when you're surrounded by several hundred other reporters trying to speak to athletes under the stand after the races end. Six or seven hours on your feet in temperatures of 100 degrees or more, made worse by television lights, is not something to take on unless you are fit. Sometimes the problems can be self-inflicted. Cramped conditions are normal rather than exceptional, and spilling the occasional litre of Coca Cola over your groin is enough to tax anybody's powers of concentration. And then there is every broadcaster's nightmare, a giggling fit. Brian Johnson must have been the arch exponent – most notably with Jonathan Agnew – but the athletics team came close in Atlanta. John Inverdale, sitting alongside me, read the sports headlines for the day with the final line about a yachting event. The gentleman's name was not quite what you wanted to hear: '...and finally a gold medal for the Brazilian, Scheidt ..., over to John,' said Inverdale as he turned away from me with tears rolling down his cheeks. I tried, pathetically, to pick up for commentary on the women's 400 metres, before being consumed by stomach-churning laughter which quickly left me mute. So it was left to Mike Whittingham to turn his back on the gigglers alongside him and somehow keep a straight face to babble some inane observation about the attributes of Marie-Jo Perec.

At the Athens World Championships in 1997, the American team in the 100 metres relay dropped the baton. Your correspondent ended with egg on his face and reduced Messrs Whittingham, Inverdale and Phillips to helpless speechlessness when he said: 'It was on the handover between the first and second legs that the Americans dropped the javelin.' Interesting alternative to a baton ... but not good for people trying to keep a straight face.

So many times people have said to me: 'Athletics sounds great on the radio. You sound as though you're having such great fun' – which, of course, is exactly what we are doing and is how we would all want it to sound. Athletics, at its best, is a wonderful expression of human endeavour and achievement. Yes, it has been sullied by those who have sought to gain unfair advantage by the use of drugs. But those who cheat are in the minority and the efforts of the governing bodies to stamp out drug abuse is to be applauded. The sadness is that the efforts of the administrators have not been supported by the law courts in certain parts of the world, leaving the situation where an athlete can be restored to competition after serving a ludicrously lenient two-year ban.

Such rules only serve to undermine the achievements of clean athletes such as Jonathan Edwards. When listeners heard Haile Gebrselassie's magnificent run for 10,000 metres gold in Athens, they were not hearing about a cheat, but about a supremely gifted man who ran with a smile on his face. Similarly, the running of the Kenyan athletes in the summer of 1997, most notably Daniel Komen, was something at which listeners could rightly marvel.

The advent of digital audio broadcasting means that the increase in the depth of athletics coverage is sure to continue, while plans are already well advanced for even more comprehensive coverage of the Olympics in Australia in the year 2000. Who will be the new heroes of the sport, to follow in the tradition of Coe and Ovett, Christie, Jackson and Gunnell? Iwan Thomas, Mark Richardson and Jamie Baulch will continue to shine in the 400 metres, Denise Lewis is looking for an Olympic gold medal in the heptathlon and perhaps Alison Curbishley can fill the void left by the retirement of Gunnell. Whoever they are, you can be sure of hearing about their deeds on the radio and learning about the personalities who make athletics such a rewarding sport to follow.

It was in Athens that Roger Black came and sat in our commentary position. After the races were over for the day, he turned to the team and said: 'You know guys, you've probably got the best job in the world.' He just might be right.

ELEANOR OLDROYD

'Only a Woman'

Eleanor Oldroyd is – so far – the only female presenter of Sports Report. *She is a former reporter on Radio One* Newsbeat *and a familiar face on Breakfast Television. Her main sporting interests are football and cricket. She is a member of the government's Football Task Force.*

Saturday 3 January 1948. The very first *Sports Report* was announced on the BBC Light Programme with the words, 'Here is Raymond Glendenning to introduce a new Saturday feature for sportsmen.' Nearly fifty years later, it was introduced for the first time by a woman.

Saturday 18 November 1995. It had been a good afternoon for Everton, at a time when good afternoons were hard to come by. They'd just enjoyed their second win in a row, following two months without one; and to make it even sweeter, it was a 2–1 win against Liverpool, at Anfield.

It had been a good afternoon for me, too – the biggest afternoon of my career. After five years of acting as a bit-player in the wonderful drama that is *Sports Report* – as a football reporter, as the voice of the 'Best of the Rest', the compilation of highlights of lower league games to which we haven't sent a reporter, as a reader of the classified racing results – I was in the hot seat at last. A succession of the most resonant male voices of the century – Eamonn Andrews, Wynford Vaughan-Thomas, Peter Jones, Desmond Lynam – and now me. I'd successfully negotiated the opening hurdles; the five o'clock headlines, the introduction of James Alexander Gordon with the football results, the dash around the country for detailed reports on our top football matches, including the commentary game, Liverpool v Everton at Anfield.

'Joe Royle's on the line from Anfield to speak to you – go to him next,' were the instructions from the producer. I expected him to be in a buoyant mood. He'd been hailed as a returning messiah when he took over as manager at Goodison, but had been under pressure after their recent poor spell. Musing out loud, I imagined the blue-clad football fans of Merseyside cramming into the pubs, big smiles on their faces, looking forward to the prospect of an evening of serious taunting of their red-clad rivals. But Joe, a football realist who'd seen it all before, would probably not be getting too carried away – after all, I put it to him, one swallow didn't make a summer, did it?

'Only a woman would ask that question.'

I'm sorry to say that I was struck dumb by his response. The obvious riposte – '*Why* Joe, would only a woman ask that question?' completely escaped me; but then you never do think of the obvious riposte until it's too late. I opened and shut my mouth several times, and allowed the interview to stagger to a bland and uneventful end.

Autumn 1991. I'm not sure exactly where it was – probably Selhurst Park, I seemed to spend an awful lot of time watching Crystal Palace and Wimbledon in those days. It was my first assignment for the greatest radio sport programme in the world. The final whistle had gone some fifteen minutes earlier, the stands had emptied, the lights had been extinguished, and then, in my headphones, I heard it. *Da-da, da-da, da-da, da-da, da-diddly-dum di-da* – instant memories of a thousand Saturday tea-times. And suddenly I was part of it. My stumbling thoughts on the match just completed about to go down in Radio Sport's journal of record; and blokes with scarves in cars driving home listening to me, saying, 'What's she on about? Was she at the game, or what?'

Now I don't suffer particularly from an inferiority complex, but when it comes to football, and especially at that sacred time, Saturday afternoon between 3 o'clock and 6 o'clock, it really is different for girls. However many women hold season tickets these days, wear their replica shirts with pride, hold forth in the pub about the merits of Shearer or Sheringham, or even present or report on *Sports Report*, there are as many men quietly convinced that football is their game, and while they'll tolerate female opinions on it, they couldn't possibly take them seriously.

The respected sports columnist Peter Corrigan sums it up when he says: 'If you were out shopping on a Saturday and desperate to know the football results, you wouldn't say, "Excuse me, madam, how did Arsenal get on?" You'd never trust a woman with something as important as a football result!'

Happily, the days have gone when a woman reporting live on a football match was as incongruous a sight as Elvis in Tesco's in Stockport. Julie Welch, who was the true pioneer when she began reporting for the *Observer* in the 1970s, remembers the dismay of a man sitting behind her at Portman Road. 'Women in the press box. So it's come to that.'

Now we're tolerated, and even in some cases, welcomed. The press stewards at Selhurst Park in particular always make a special point of making sure a cup of tea and some sandwiches are held back for those of us who can't dash straight down to the press room on the half-time whistle, because we're way down the reporting pecking order behind those at the lofty meccas of Old Trafford, Highbury and Anfield. Press facilities are not designed with women in mind; in the cramped conditions at the average ground, I would never dream of wearing anything other than trousers; mini-skirts and high-heeled boots (*de rigueur* for players' girlfriends and chairmen's wives) are hardly practical if you find yourself scrambling over neighbouring seats and rickety desks to make your way to your assigned spot.

When it comes to seeking the after-match comments of the main protagonists, again matters have improved. Women are now allowed to do interviews in the tunnel at White Hart Lane, but this was a concession which required an epic battle between Charlotte Nicol, the first female football reporter on *Sports*

Report, and the Tottenham hierarchy. Permission was finally granted by the Spurs chairman Alan Sugar; but only on condition that Charlotte would promise to stand in a spot which prevented her having any view of semi-clad players. The American system of the locker-room interview is most definitely not encouraged at the football grounds of Great Britain; although some of my most embarrassing moments as a sports broadcaster came in my local radio days, covering the local ice hockey team, the Telford Tigers. Keen to follow in the North American tradition, their coach took to inviting me into the dressing room after key matches.

Rather than reaching for items of clothing to cover their modesty, as you might expect, the players decided they were going to do everything in their power to put me off, and as towels were merrily cast aside all around me I found myself concentrating very hard on asking relevant questions and gazing fixedly into the eyes of my interviewee. It's probably a blessed relief that football has never tried to emulate ice hockey; the smell of sweat and the brush of damp jockstraps hanging from the ceiling never particularly added to the authenticity of the interview, I found.

So I'm happy to wait until players or managers are showered and decently dressed before asking them for their words of wisdom. Generally speaking, players and the younger generation of managers will treat the female interviewer pretty much as an equal; their more senior counterparts sometimes find it necessary to exert their masculinity, to remind the imposter of her true standing in the football hierarchy.

After one Premiership match, I was patiently waiting to seek the considered views of the manager – a well-known former England player. When he finally emerged from entertaining the club's sponsors, I was waiting for him in a busy corridor, surrounded by fellow hacks and banging doors, so I requested that we might be able to find a quieter spot to record the interview. Immediately an arm went round my shoulders – 'Can we go somewhere quieter? Of course we can, darling – just you come with me! And if we're not back in half an hour, lads – don't bother coming looking for us!'

Sadly, the preferred reaction to such an invitation (the quick kick in the shins or somewhere even more delicate) is not an option in these circumstances; you never know when you (or a colleague) might need to interview the same manager again. So all I could do was laugh merrily, grit my teeth, and make a rapid exit as soon as the interview was completed.

As well as being *Sports Report*'s first female football reporter, Charlotte Nicol went on to become Radio Sport's first female football producer. She has had her fair share of brushes with senior footballing figures untouched by the magic wand of political correctness. One high profile chairman asked her as she arrived at a media gathering whether she was there for the press conference, or if she'd come to pour the drinks. A year or so later Charlotte felt she'd made progress when he referred to her – the person responsible for co-ordinating all Radio Five Live's football coverage – as 'that charming PA'.

Bastions are being assaulted then, but true parity with the men is still some way off, I fear. As I write this, I have just received a letter from a listener who, while 'wishing me well in the future', opined that I and other female football presenters should 'get back to *Woman's Hour*', and stop intruding on a game 'invented by men, for men'. Such missives are outnumbered considerably by positive messages of support and congratulation; but every time I report from a football match, my mind goes back to the fictional male fan in his car shouting at his radio. Any mistake I make will, I'm convinced, be judged much more harshly than the same mistake made by a man. I always neurotically read the report of the match I've covered in the Sunday papers the next morning, to check if their correspondents agree with my assessment of the match.

And do women see football in a different light from men? A question which I've frequently been asked, but find hard to answer. There are differences, I'm sure; all the male football obsessives of my acquaintance have an extraordinary ability to recall statistics. Run down their team's fixture list of the previous season, and they can tell you precisely score, scorers and even time of goals. Whereas I struggle to remember matches I've been to just a fortnight before; as witness the fact

that the details of my first game for *Sports Report* are distinctly
not imprinted on my brain.

Yet my emotions are influenced by the beautiful game more
powerfully than by any sport, or form of entertainment. I went
to Italy and marvelled at the (sadly fleeting) talents of Paul
Gascoigne at the 1990 World Cup, I cried with happiness when
Arsenal grittily hung on to a 1–0 lead to win the European Cup
Winners Cup in 1994. I'm no different from any football fan,
male or female; I just have the good fortune to earn a living
talking about it.

For a large part of the last fifty years, women have had a role
on *Sports Report*, even if for the most part it has been unseen
and unsung. I feel immensely privileged to have been the first to
take on the mantle worn by so many of the broadcasting
legends, and hope I will be allowed to do so for many more
years. And after female presenters, producers and reporters,
what next for women and radio sport's flagship show? 'With
live second-half commentary from Stamford Bridge – Michelle
Ingham and Alannah Green'? *Sports Report* may be closer to its
centenary than its diamond jubilee before that happens. But I
very much doubt that in 1948, Angus Mackay could have
envisaged a female Raymond Glendenning, or imagined that
his brainchild would become a friend to sportswomen as much
as to sportsmen.

HARRY CARPENTER

Harry's Game: Fifty Years of Boxing

Confidant of Ali, Bruno and Cooper and commentator on a whole lexicon of boxers before and since, Harry Carpenter has been a Sports Report *contributor since the early days. He also presented golf, tennis and Olympic Games coverage for BBC Television, and now lives in retirement in France.*

So 50 years of boxing – and of my life – have passed since *Sports Report* first went on the air. In that time, not surprisingly, both of us have changed beyond recognition.

Never mind about my life. That's already been reviewed in a book I have no intention of rewriting. Let's look at some of the things that have happened in boxing. Might as well get the old man's prejudice out of the way early on. I know boxing has always been a business as well as a sport. Can I just express the view that over the years it has swayed much more towards money and much further away from sport? At the top level, anyway. And it's none the better for it. Young supporters of the game can now mutter 'silly old b...' and move along to some other part of the book. Goodbye.

The most interesting thing I discovered when I took a look at the files for January 1948 is that British boxing had only recently abolished the colour bar. Those young people who have stopped reading this might not even know what a colour bar is, it all seems so impossible now.

Simply put, it meant that if you weren't white, you couldn't fight for a British title. Hands up in horror! But that's the way it was until the autumn of 1947 and in my searches, through files and my own memories, I can find no indication that there was any huge public demand in Britain to have the colour-bar rescinded. Yet we were accustomed to applauding black champions ... in another country.

At that time, half a century ago, the most popular and best known boxer in the world was Joe Louis, a black man who had been heavyweight champion of the world for a decade and had made more than 20 successful defences of his title. He was the first black sportsman to overcome racial prejudice in the USA. Did you know, incidentally, that it was not until the late 1940s that a black American was allowed to take his place in a major league baseball team?

There had been only one previous black world heavyweight champion: Jack Johnson, of Texas, champion from 1908 to 1915, who outraged America because (a) he had destroyed the comfortable image of white supremacy, and (b) had married a white woman. This liaison eventually brought about his banishment from the USA and after 1912 he never defended his title in his own country.

Once Johnson had been vanquished (in Cuba) by the white American Jess Willard in 1915, no black man fought for the world heavyweight title again until Joe Louis came along in 1937. Set against this wider background, the British colour-bar which lasted until 1947 may not seem so outlandish.

It was abolished without fuss and surprisingly little publicity by the British Boxing Board of Control with a major rewrite of their Regulation 31, paragraph 4, which, until then, had stated that 'contestants for a British title must be legally British subjects and born of white parents.'

The new version said: 'A contestant must be a British subject who was born and is normally resident and domiciled in the United Kingdom, and whose father was himself a British subject at the time of the contestant's birth and domiciled in the United Kingdom.'

Until this change black boxers in Britain could only challenge for the British Empire (!) title, while any white boxer from the Dominions could fight for a British title, even though he didn't live here. Hence, we had a white South African, Ben Foord, as British heavyweight champion from 1936 to 1937.

So, in January 1948, *Sports Report* made its debut slap in the middle of this major shake-up in British boxing and precisely 30 days after that first broadcast Dick Turpin, son of a black father and white mother, became the first coloured man to become involved in a British championship when he beat Mark Hart of Croydon in a final eliminator for the middleweight title in Nottingham. Later that year, Turpin beat Vince Hawkins to become Britain's first coloured champion.

Note my use of the word 'coloured'. Here's another change in the way we look at things. In 1948 it was considered totally insulting to refer to anyone as 'black'. The polite term was 'coloured'. In 1998 the reverse is true.

Dick Turpin, from Leamington Spa, was the elder brother of the eventually more famous Randolph, also a middleweight, who enlivened the early years of *Sports Report* by laying out rivals from Europe and the USA with some of the most dramatic punching ever seen in a British ring. Without that timely change in British boxing law, these remarkable brothers, the quietly methodical Dick and the ferociously exciting Randy, might have languished in the hinterland of Empire titles.

As it was, Randolph graduated from British to European titles to win the world middleweight championship from the legendary Sugar Ray Robinson of America on a July 1951 night at Earls Court, London, when 18,000 hysterically aroused people, myself among them, stood and sang 'For He's A Jolly Good Fellow' after Turpin's victory. That day was the best any British sport had experienced in the years immediately after World War Two.

With or without your permission, I intend to drag you away for a moment from professional boxing to amateur. I can't remember whether *Sports Report* devoted much time to amateur boxing. Probably not. Hardly anyone did, apart from BBC Television. And the only reason for that was the refusal of the British Boxing Board to allow professional boxing to be televised in the years we are discussing.

All my early TV commentaries were devoted to amateur boxing, and what a harvest we reaped. There was the remarkably elongated Bruce Wells, a man of 11 stone who stood some 6 feet 3 inches tall, with the ensuing beanpole of a reach. Bruce won a European title and became very famous.

So did Wild Willie Bannon from Scotland with a style that owed nothing to technique, everything to enthusiasm. I always made a point of stressing a boxer's occupation, and Willie, or Wullie as the Scots called him, became nationally recognised as the Dundee coal-heaver.

My old mate Roy Francis, today a respected international professional referee, still winces when I remind him that in the days when he was knocking out Americans at Wembley he was known as the Brixton eel-skinner.

The impact of amateur boxing on TV in those days was such that people still talk to me about the November night in 1961 when Great Britain whitewashed the USA 10–0 at Wembley. Billy Walker, the West Ham fish porter, achieved superstar status when he sent a huge heavyweight, Cornelius Perry (Philadelphia baker), crashing out in the opening round.

From that win sprang Billy's well-paid conversion to professionalism, under brother George's management, and from the money they earned together grew the mammoth financial empire of Brent Walker. How about that for romance?

It has become accepted legend that Billy's KO capped the evening and gave us the clean sweep. Not true. BBC TV had asked for a change in the order of contests to make sure Billy Walker's contest would be seen on the box (everything was live in those days. Videotape? …never heard of it). The Walker-Perry bout was actually No. 7 of the evening.

Hands up those who can tell me who made it 10–0. Give in? It was the Coventry light-middleweight Derek Richards. He stopped his man in the second round. It really was an amazing night and all ten of our men deserve a re-mention. The Great Britain team that memorably slapped the Yanks was: Fly: Alan Rudkin. Bantam: Peter Bennyworth. Feather: Frankie Taylor. Light: Dick McTaggart. Light-welter: Brian Brazier. Welter: Jim Lloyd. Light-middle: Derek Richards. Middle: John Fisher. Light-heavy: Dennis Pollard. Heavy: Billy Walker. Well done, lads.

You see the name Dick McTaggart in there. He was still boxing – and winning – five years after he'd collected Olympic gold at Melbourne in 1956. Dick, the Dundee rat-catcher, is the only amateur of my time who won every championship he entered, from RAF to Olympic Games. In 1960 he went to the Rome Olympics and came away with a bronze. Today, unfortunately, amateur boxing is almost totally ignored by the media, television included. If there is another Dick McTaggart around, he is doomed to remain unsung.

One more recollection of the amateurs: the triumph of Chris Finnegan in the 1968 Olympic Games in Mexico City. BBC TV obviously wanted to interview him after his win, which was late at night. The only way it could be done was to get him out of the stadium and into the television studios the BBC were occupying about a mile away. From there he would be interviewed from London over the satellite, which was costing heaven knows how many hundreds of pounds a minute to keep open and which would pass beyond use within an hour or so.

Getting Chris out of that stadium was a problem, because he'd been selected to provide a urine test, a matter of some difficulty for him as he'd become completely dehydrated winning his Olympic gold against a formidable Russian. Taps were turned on to encourage him, to no avail, at which point my BBC producers, Slim Wilkinson and Bob Duncan, became extremely agitated, knowing that time was running out, even if nothing else was. They raised their voices to such effect that the medical staff surrounding Finnegan agreed to let him go to the studios, provided they could accompany him and, sooner or later, get their specimen.

Finding a taxi was out of the question, so at around midnight a small army of harassed men were seen running through the streets of Mexico City: Finnegan, the bricklayer from Hayes, Middlesex, leading the way, tracksuited, gold medal swinging from his neck; Wilkinson, puffing hard, but determined not to lose his man; Duncan, backing up admirably; myself, whingeing and wheezing, wondering what I'd done to deserve this on top of a night's hard commentating; and, at the rear, two white-coated medical men, one of them clutching the specimen bottle.

We made it in time for the satellite interview, but Chris still couldn't do the works. We moved on to the restaurant where the British team were celebrating Finnegan's win and, as he took his place at the top table, a very large jug of beer was placed before him.

Shortly after 2 a.m. Chris got to his feet, a touch unsteadily, and announced proudly: 'I think I'm ready to go now,' and accompanied the medics to the gents. The result was negative, but my memory of that night was extremely positive.

Let's move back a year or two, to February 1964, and Miami Beach. As far as I know, this was the first time *Sports Report* had been presented entirely from abroad. The man at the mike in Miami, of course, was the incomparable Eamonn Andrews and I was his sidekick for the occasion. Back in London producer Angus Mackay masterminded the operation.

The core of the programme was the imminent clash for the world heavyweight title between the champion, Sonny Liston, and his precocious challenger, Cassius Clay. All week Eamonn and I had been out and about collecting interviews and opinions, but the over-riding magic of the programme was that Eamonn, in a Miami studio, was able to feed in the day's entire news from Britain and introduce all the soccer reports. This was achieved by the simple mechanics of my putting on a set of headphones, scribbling down the information Angus was barking into my ear from London, and slipping it to Eamonn for transmission. Sounds primitive and it was. But it worked and it was typical of the programme's constant willingness to stretch its format to the limits.

Clay – soon to become Muhammad Ali – was a 7–1 outsider in this fight, which may seem unbelievable at this point in history, but was perfectly understandable at the time. Liston, a brooding brute of a man, the Mike Tyson of his time, had only ever lost one fight, and that having fought seven of the eight rounds with a broken jaw. Clay was perceived as a bizarrely talented whippersnapper, who could move nicely, but whose mouth was considerably larger than his ability. Against Liston he would surely get what was coming to him.

The only person I knew – apart from Clay – who refused to go along with this scenario was Eamonn, who maintained doggedly that Clay was precisely what he claimed to be, a whole new thing in heavyweight boxing and that his personality, allied to brilliant skill, would overcome the lumbering, old-fashioned Liston.

And so it turned out, although not before Clay had pleaded to be let out of the fight because something had got into his eyes. His trainer, Angelo Dundee, told him not to be silly (or words to that effect) and shoved him back into the ring, whereupon the ogre Liston plumped down on his stool after six rounds and said HE couldn't go on because his shoulder hurt. Ah, the mysterious manoeuvres of boxing...

Eamonn certainly was prophetic, because Clay – Muhammad Ali – went on to change the face of heavyweight boxing and provided the world with years of entertainment, in and out of the ring, which is nowhere being matched today.

The most talked about fighter now is Mike Tyson, but he is not entertaining, just morbidly fascinating with his finger constantly on the self-destruct button. I fear for him. Yet my own experience of the man is far from unpleasant. Quite the reverse.

In 1987, when he already held two of the world's three major heavyweight titles, he came to London and agreed to join me in a BBC TV editing suite where we had gathered reels of old film showing past heavyweight champions, going back to the early days of the century. We put a mike on Tyson (sorry!), plonked him in a chair in front of the editing machine and had our own *Sportsnight* camera trained on him. I then ran through the reels of old-time fighters and invited him to comment. He knew something about all of them and offered decisive opinions on their ability, from Jess Willard to Floyd Patterson. It was a masterly performance, with no semblance of a script and no rehearsal. We showed it on *Sportsnight* as an insight into Tyson's hidden persona and it caused huge interest.

The reason he was so knowledgeable was that one of his managers, Jim Jacobs, had been a collector of old fight films and Tyson had spent countless hours studying them in Jacobs' apartment in New York. I asked Mike who was the best of all the old-time fighters he had seen on film and he came up with the astounding reply that it was Owen Moran, of Birmingham, England, a featherweight who was around before World War One.

During that week in March, 1987, he sat beside me at the Wembley ringside and helped me cover the Frank Bruno-James Tillis fight. He identified some flaws in Bruno's defence and clearly kept them in mind for the two fights he later had with Frank. I try very hard to hold on to these memories when I read about Mike's descents into manic – and criminal – assault. Maybe there are some excuses...

His early life in one of Brooklyn's foulest slums was one of appalling deprivation. The men responsible for dragging him out of the gutter – Cus D'Amato and Jim Jacobs – died while he was still shaping his career. The marriage to Robin Givens was a hideous disaster, which cost him a sizeable part of his fortune and, I would guess, part of his reason. He has been adrift on an ocean of dollars with no one to steer him for too many years. The cynicism with which he is handled has eaten into the very fabric of heavyweight boxing.

It rubs off, too, on the man in the street. I cannot tell you the number of otherwise sane human beings who commented to me, after Tyson had chewed a lump out of Evander Holyfield's ear, that 'they'll make even more money in the third fight.' Well, if that is the way big-time boxing is viewed in 1998, I am delighted to be out of it.

I'll stick with my happy relationship with Frank Bruno, who came so fortuitously into my life just as Muhammad Ali was dropping out of it in 1980, when Frank won the ABA (amateur) heavyweight title. He got a points decision over the Welshman,

Rudi Pika, and Frank likes to rub it in that I didn't agree with it. He's right, but then we all have our off-nights. Maybe we both did on that occasion.

It's fashionable today to say that Frank's pro career was built on a succession of no-hopers who folded quickly. I'd like to point out that when you have a punch like Frank's, in either hand, and you land it on the other gentleman's whiskers, anyone can look like a no-hoper. We should celebrate the fact that, in Frank, Britain had her best heavyweight hitter since Henry Cooper and in the 50 years of *Sports Report* I haven't seen any better.

I've had a lot of good times with big Frank, like the day he got married and wildly excited onlookers clambered on to the roofs of houses to get a better look at him and his bride Laura as they left the church. And like the night we performed before the Queen at the London Palladium in the Royal Variety Performance.

We did a cross-talk act and after the show lined up on the stage with Jerry Lewis, Tina Turner, Edward Woodward and the rest of the performers for the traditional inspection by Her Majesty. Frank and I were centre stage, second row, behind the undoubted stars of the night, a team of Argentine bolo-swingers. The Queen stopped and had a chat with them, just in front of us. She then moved on and before she had gone a yard, Frank boomed out, in that foghorn of a voice: ' 'Arry, she's blown you out!' It was no good. She didn't come back.

Just to return to that business of Britain abolishing her boxing colour-bar, thus giving black boxers their natural rights. In all the 15 years Frank Bruno was a professional, he never once boxed for the British title. Now there's irony for you.

PETER BAXTER

Cricket in the 1980s: Ian Botham

Peter Baxter is the BBC's cricket producer and custodian since 1973 of Test Match Special. In a long BBC career, Peter has also produced rugby union and for many years masterminded radio's coverage of the Boat Race. He is the author of several books inspired by TMS.

The BBC first sent me to report on an England cricket tour in 1981. Within my first few days of assimilating this unusual way of life, I found myself with the team in Ahmedabad, in the west of India. As tends to happen on an afternoon when the practice session is complete and time is hanging heavy, we asked the question, 'What is the local attraction for sight-seeing?' 'The Shaking Towers', we were told.

These turned out to be a pair of minarets at a small local mosque. A mixed party of players and press was assembled to visit this curiosity. On arrival we saw that one of the minarets was little more than a stump, but the other still stood against the dust-laden sky. 'They don't shake at all,' proclaimed the first pair to climb the stairs.

'I'll make the so-and-so's shake,' said Ian Botham. And he did. Now I looked at the broken-off minaret. Had our Beefy been this way before?

Also on that tour, before a match in Indore, Botham

announced that he was bored and that he might decide to have some fun when he batted. He was only at the crease for 55 minutes, but in that time he made 122 with the aid of seven sixes and then stalked off to play a furious game of badminton.

That was the energy of Ian Terence Botham, which in 1980 the selectors, on the suggestion of Mike Brearley, had decided to harness in the England captaincy. It was not a successful enterprise, though it should be noted that, of his twelve Tests in charge, nine were against the might of the West Indies and the other three against Australia. His captaincy record was lost 4, drew 8, but no wins.

Botham's resignation as captain seemed to let the genie out of the bottle. The very next Test, the third of the 1981 series, saw him take six Australian wickets in the first innings and then, in an England batting debacle, be the only one to reach fifty. But England were following on and still needing 122 to avoid an innings defeat with half the side out when he came in to bat. It got worse. They were 92 behind when the seventh wicket fell, but that was when Botham got into his stride. Yes, he needed luck, but his exhibition of hitting first amused and then electrified the country. 149 not out at the end of the innings, he had given England a slender glimpse of daylight and it was enough of a chink for Bob Willis to force it open and wrench an improbable victory.

Australia had failed by 18 runs to reach the modest target of 130. A fortnight later we were at Edgbaston and they had reached 114 for 5, needing only 151 in total. Mike Brearley tossed the ball to a reluctant Botham. In 28 balls, keeping the ball well up at a lively pace, he took those last five wickets at a personal cost of just one run. In Wisden's words, the Australian batsmen '"walked into the point of the lance'.

Nor had The Great Botham Summer finished. At Old Trafford, when England seemed to be losing their way in the attempt to build on a first innings lead, Botham reached a century from 86 balls (one fewer than he had needed at Headingley the previous month). His hooking Dennis Lillee with the new ball for six remains a legend, as does the applause that that great fast bowler awarded the shot. The gigantic deeds that went before dictate that few ever mention the ten wickets he took in the drawn final Test of that summer.

Botham himself rates that 1981 Old Trafford century one of his two best. The other came five years later in Brisbane, when England had been written off by Australians and by their own travelling media party. Botham the defiant rammed home his message when England had been put in, at his best showing the fledgling Phillip DeFreitas the ropes. Throughout that tour Botham played his part, in fact, a part not always reflected in the figures, which involved him staying out of a limelight which always seemed to seek him out, on and off the field during his career.

It led him into trouble when he was banned for half a season for too frank an admission about earlier experiments with cannabis, but, typically, he returned to Test cricket with a wicket off his first ball. It seemed that the batsman, Bruce Edgar of New Zealand, was hypnotised by the enormous aura and expectation of the Botham reputation.

In that match in 1986, Botham became the world's leading Test wicket-taker, relieving Dennis Lillee of the title. For all the self-belief that had characterised his career, it was quite touching that he seemed almost embarrassed to have overtaken such a great bowler. His final haul of 383 Test wickets has since been surpassed, in turn, but add those to his 5,200 runs from 102 Tests, with 14 centuries, and you have a record surpassed only by Kapil Dev. Botham can add to his tally 120 catches – mostly at slip. This was a remarkable cricketer.

Botham the hell-raiser needed to have fun and sometimes authority found it hard to stomach. Sometimes, indeed, some of his friends found it hard to defend his brand of fun. But what could never be denied was the generosity of spirit that led him to undertake his various walks for leukaemia research, the most remarkable, perhaps, the first, from John O'Groats to Land's End. Those who may have dismissed it as a publicity stunt might reflect, did Ian Botham really need the publicity?

He emerged from the 1970s and ended his career as Durham's crowd-puller in the 1990s, but the 1980s were his decade. There was no surer way of emptying a bar at a cricket ground, of getting the family in from the garden to watch the television, or of adding a yard of pace to your stride to the county ground's turnstiles than the words, 'Botham's in.'

MAGIC MOMENTS...

Life out in the field appears to be a glamorous one. Roll up to the best sporting events in the world, sit in a comfortable commentary box with an unimpaired view, enjoy the sponsor's hospitality, and then tell the nation what you think from time to time.

In reality, it's not quite like that. Take Roddy Forsyth, for example, who was in mid-flow from Tynecastle when his script was 'vandalised' by a pigeon – who needed a comfort break.

Or Pat Murphy, who was delivering his finely-honed script from the Hawthorns one bleak November evening when somebody decided to turn the lights off in the stand. Not easy to switch onto auto-pilot at a moment's notice.

JIMMY ARMFIELD

The Rise and Rise of Manchester United

Jimmy Armfield played more than 600 games for Blackpool, won 43 England caps and managed both Bolton and Leeds; he continues to be involved in the game as a consultant to the Football Association. A Sports Report *regular for nearly 20 years, Jimmy also presents his own series of* Football Legends.

Manchester United were the first team to make me realise that there was football life beyond Blackpool's South Pier. And as they claimed their fourth Premiership title out of the last five in 1997, they were also the last English team to make me believe that we can still produce teams to take on the world. In five decades Manchester United have simply become one of our great sporting clubs, known worldwide and watched by millions.

Their rise from a bombed-out soccer stadium, during the last war, to a stockmarket giant has been nothing short of incredible, and for a football fanatic like me who was actually born in Manchester, but reared in Blackpool, the word 'United' can mean only one thing.

Before the War, the club had its moments, but frankly neighbours City across Manchester were as big and often bigger as they paraded stars like the great Frank Swift and Peter

Doherty – incidentally the former born in Blackpool, the latter bought from Blackpool!

Ironically, it was an ex-City man who really put Manchester United on the map: his name, Matt Busby, a Scottish wing half who was on the Maine Road staff when they won the FA Cup in the mid-1930s. Busby was the man who set the pattern as he inherited one team, built another, and bought a third which took United to heights they could never have dreamed of as football returned to normal after hostilities ceased in 1945. The genial Scot was a man who believed in letting talent have its head, but all within the framework of the unit. He had balanced teams, and yet each one of them was fired by stars who could produce the out-of-the-ordinary when needed.

So it was on that May day back in 1948 when United had the audacity to beat Blackpool 4–2 in one of the great Wembley FA Cup Finals. By then I was living in Blackpool, and as a 12-year-old boy I was on the kop at Wembley shouting for the Seasiders, who with Matthews, Mortensen and Johnston were surely unbeatable. Tottenham, the soccer purists from the capital, had been swept aside at Villa Park in the semi-final, so Manchester United were set to become another notch on the belt and our Stan would at last get his Cup medal.

We were 2–1 up, and as my father and I ate our sandwiches at half time we were preparing for the celebrations along the Golden Mile. The next 45 minutes changed everything, and probably my whole life too. As I stood on the biscuit tin which had held our sandwiches (I was always a bit small as a lad) I was transfixed as I watched United, in their blue shirts, move the ball across the hallowed turf with a style I hadn't seen before.

I was sad at defeat, but for the first time I actually started to think about the balance of a football team and why it was that United looked so superior. It was a combination of talent and movement, with and without the ball – something that Busby took with him throughout his career. The second half at Wembley that day gave Busby his first trophy as a manager and so began the legend of the man and his club. I can name his United side without prompting: Crompton; Carey, Aston; Anderson, Chilton, Cockburn; Delany, Morris, Rowley,

Pearson and Mitten. Eleven players who provided the base which now supports one of the world's great sporting institutions. Busby had 'arrived', and from that point United have never looked back.

They have had their ups and downs with the rest, there have been tragedies, heartaches and disappointments, yet along the way they have had many, many more prize moments to cherish. The enigmatic talent of George Best is still talked about today, there was quicksilver Denis Law, as sharp as a needle in the box, and Nobby Stiles – toothless in the head, but never in the tackle.

Then there was the great talent of Bobby Charlton, a Busby Babe who survived Munich and led the team to its greatest moment. A player who could lift the crowd with one thunderbolt shot and inspire his colleagues with his energy, pace and technical ability. In my opinion, he is the most influential footballer we have had since the war, and I doubt whether England would have won the World Cup in 1966 without him. Charlton is United through and through, and is still involved today in the Old Trafford boardroom.

There have been some wonderful moments over the years, and from the BBC commentary position I still get that tingle of excitement every time we cover a big game at 'The Shrine', as Stuart Hall often calls it. Yet as a boy in Manchester, my earliest recollections of Manchester United were a bit vague. They were the team without a ground, as a direct hit from a German bomb meant Old Trafford was out of use, and so Busby and his team were forced to ground-share with neighbours City at Maine Road once hostilities had ceased. But even that didn't check their surge to the top. In the first five seasons after the war, United finished runners-up four times before dropping to fourth in 1950. They moved back to Old Trafford, won the Cup, and then in 1951–52 took the title as well as they paraded a brand of football that captivated the soccer lovers of this country.

It was that team which put United on to the football map in a big way. But it was the players who followed that really made Busby into a soccer legend and gave the club the worldwide following it has today. In the mid-1950s United uncovered probably the best crop of young players ever to emerge from the same club at one time. The Busby Babes swept through English football at whirlwind speed. Within twelve months of them arriving on the football scene in 1955, they had won the Championship, repeating the feat a year later – then tragically they had their world taken away from them in the Munich air disaster of February 1958. Looking back, it all seemed to happen so quickly. One minute they were destined to be champions of Europe then they were gone. That's how I remember it.

Busby's second great team in a decade – the Babes – were in my opinion the best side United have produced since the war. That is why their loss left such a gulf in English football. Players like Duncan Edwards, Roger Byrne and Tommy Taylor were key players in the England team, and others like Eddie Colman and David Pegg were surely destined for the big scene as well. Pegg, like Colman, Byrne, Edwards, Foulkes, Jones, Whelan and Viollet had all come through the ranks, and right behind them were Bobby Charlton, Wilf McGuinness, Colin Webster and Albert Scanlon, who all come to the fore after Munich.

Over the years, great names have been easier to recall in connection with Manchester United rather than great games or great victories. Maybe that is because there have been so many of the latter, but of the really great footballers few were better than Duncan Edwards. I know looking back it's easy to exaggerate or overstate a point, but even today I still rate my pal 'Big Dunc' as one of the best I ever saw. His achievements speak for themselves: at 16 he was in United's team, and by the time he had reached 18 he was a regular in the England side. He was built like a boxer, around 6 feet tall and 13 stones, and he possessed a powerful running style that could see him in defence one minute then surging into attack the next.

But it wasn't all about power and strength. Duncan had a wonderful touch on the ball, and it has always been my belief that Munich robbed our game of one of its greatest-ever talents. Eight of United's players were killed on that fateful day as the team returned victorious from their European Cup quarter-final success in Belgrade. It was a moment that I will never forget. I suppose the only parallel I can offer is that it was probably how an American would have felt on the day that John Kennedy was assassinated. The Babes were my contemporaries: Edwards, Colman and Foulkes were on National Service at the same time as I, and we played together in the British Army team, while I met Taylor, Pegg and Byrne on England duty. Overall they were a terrific team, and looking back probably our greatest-ever achievement at Blackpool came in 1956 when we finished runners-up to United in the Championship.

We will never know where or how far that team could have gone. But after Munich there was an incredible wave of sympathy, support, call it what you will, towards United, and just as in 1945 (following the bomb blast on Old Trafford) the club still managed to prise something out of tragedy.

That spirit of United was in fact never more evident than in the last few months of that season. Incredibly, 13 days after the crash, with Busby still in a Munich hospital, assistant manager Jimmy Murphy put out a team to face Sheffield Wednesday in an FA Cup tie. I recall they had to leave blanks in the programme team sheet, because Murphy was never sure who would be able to play. United won 3–0, and on a tide of emotion that year they reached Wembley, picking up experienced players like Ernie Taylor and Stan Crowther to help the United reserves who were thrust into the action through necessity.

The Cup, though, eluded them – Nat Lofthouse and Bolton were too strong for a patched-up United. But United won more than the Cup that year. They won the hearts of many people who hadn't followed football before, and of course when Busby returned they set out on the chase to find football's Holy Grail – the European Cup. Busby's dream had to come true. Somehow I always felt he was a man who wrote his own headlines. There was an inevitability about it.

Yet no one ever hands you a big prize – it has to be won, and Matt Busby had the know-how to put together a side that could beat the best in Europe. He did it, too, without one of his brightest stars – Denis Law, who missed out on the big day against Benfica at Wembley. But a young Brian Kidd stepped off the production line to score in the Final, and with George Best and Bobby Charlton at their sparkling best English football witnessed one of its greatest nights. United do produce moments like that, they have done for 50 years, and I have the feeling that there are still more to come.

Towards the end of my playing career in the early 1970s, United did dip out of the top flight for the only time since the War. Looking back, it seems incredible that it could happen. Yet in 1973 the writing was on the wall as United finished 18th, with only 37 points from 42 matches in Division One. The following year they ended with five points less, three places further down, and were dumped into Division Two for the first time in 36 years. Even then there was a sensational ending to their life at the top – incredibly it was a goal from Denis Law (who had been transferred to Manchester City) that put United down. Over 50,000 Mancunians were there to see it, and it was a day that few of them will ever forget.

One label that can never be tagged on to United is 'Second Class' – and in fact within twelve months they had won the Second Division title and were bouncing back towards another FA Cup success two years later. High profile managers like Tommy Docherty and Ron Atkinson assured United of headlines and some talented players as well. Docherty's Cup winners of 1977 were an all-action line-up that linked well, had pace down the flanks and played with real flair and imagination. They beat my Leeds United team in the semi-final 2–1, and the confidence they had built up saw them shock favourites Liverpool at Wembley.

This was probably one of the few successful United teams that lacked a real superstar. There were some top-class players like Coppell, Pearson, the Greenhoff brothers, Buchan and Macari, but it was the overall speed and running off the ball that made this a real team. Oddly, this side never looked like Championship material. It couldn't sustain the form it showed in Cup football. And yet it was one of the best sides we produced in the 1970s, at a time when Liverpool were settling in as the kings of English and often European soccer.

For a while, United had to play second fiddle as Shankly, Paisley and Fagan took the tiller at Anfield and steered their ship to successive Championships. United bought Bryan Robson and Ray Wilkins, but it took the arrival of another Scot – Alex Ferguson – to get the show back on the road. Even he had a difficult two years, and it took all of Chairman Martin Edwards' resolve to hold on at a crucial time when Fergie and his team were experiencing tension-packed days. But it proved to be worthwhile, and in the last few years United have surged back to the top with Cup and League successes, ventures into Europe, big-name players, a flotation on the stock market and full houses for every game at Old Trafford.

Yet another title success in 1997, and with the ever-increasing need for money to stay on top of the football tree, United do look in prime position to dominate English football. They possess another crop of youngsters – Beckham, Butt, Cole, Scholes, Giggs and the Neville brothers – who suggest that Ferguson, like Busby, may one day claim his Holy Grail as well. Certainly United target such prizes: some clubs are happy just to be in the top half of the Premiership, but that could never be enough for United.

The demands of playing at such a club are enormous, and it takes an experienced campaigner like Alex Ferguson to handle it all – not just for himself, but for his players as well. Alex once told me that a big part of his job was to teach his players, when they join the club, what it actually means to play for Manchester United. Every game is crucial: the fans expect the best. I recall when Fergie was forced to play a weakened team in a League Cup match, one member of the media commented that United would be glad to be out of the competition. Ferguson replied: 'This is Manchester United, we don't go out to do anything but win. Everybody wants to beat us, and we know it. That is the challenge every player in this club faces week in and week out, whether he plays in the first team or the youth side.' That is how I have always seen United as well.

They have always attracted the best players, and over the years they have provided some of the best players to wear an England shirt. Edwards, Charlton, Stiles, Robson ... the list is endless, and if last summer's Le Tournoi in France is anything to go by, then there could be others ready to follow in the footsteps of those who have graced the game.

My last game in League football was against Manchester United. We drew 1–1 at Bloomfield Road and I couldn't think of a better way of going out than that. Yet it could all have been so different, as in November 1957 Matt Busby tried to buy me from Blackpool – but our manager Joe Smith wouldn't let me go, and in those days 'no' meant 'never'.

Had I gone to Old Trafford, I could easily have been on that plane coming back from Munich just three months later.

SIMON TAYLOR

From Hunt to Hill

Simon Taylor was BBC Radio Sport's motor-racing commentator for 20 years, spanning the World Championship triumphs of James Hunt in 1976 and Damon Hill in 1996. No slouch behind the wheel himself, Simon is a publisher by profession and a classic cars enthusiast.

Grand Prix motor-racing is nowadays a worldwide sport of the first rank, so it seems hard to realise that only 40 years ago it was merely a fringe activity for the wealthy, which rarely featured on the sports pages of the newspapers. If Stirling Moss won a great victory for Britain overseas, it was normally tucked away on the foreign news pages, and only lurid fatal accidents – which, in those days of scant concern for driver and circuit safety, were by no means infrequent – were given headline treatment.

Nevertheless, BBC Radio's coverage of motor-racing had been growing steadily ever since, in June 1932, it put out the first-ever live outside broadcast of a motor-sporting event: the rather parochial Shelsley Walsh hillclimb in Worcestershire. Twenty years later, in my 1950s childhood, I listened spellbound to racing coverage from converted wartime airfields like Silverstone and Goodwood, with wizard-prang commentary provided by the formidable trio of Raymond Baxter, Robin Richards and John Bolster.

Wartime RAF pilot Baxter, as senior commentator, was

always positioned near the start-finish line, with Richards 'out in the country' half-way round the lap. Bolster, lugging the back pack and other heavy equipment necessary in those days to allow a roving reporter to do his job on-air, was stationed in the pits, ready to describe the refuelling stops and the breakdowns, and interview the drivers after the race. Bolster had been a successful racing driver himself until a major accident in 1949 ended his career, and his breezy tones and striking figure – luxuriant moustache, loud check jacket, matching deerstalker hat – became a familiar part of the British motor-racing scene.

Of course, the post-race interviews were all rather restrained and gentlemanly. There was no winner's podium in those days: a trophy would normally be handed over to the hot, dirty driver on the finish line by somebody's wife. There might be a chaste, oily kiss for the cameras, but any champagne would be carefully drunk rather than carelessly sprayed.

Although major countries had named their premier races 'Grand Prix' ever since motor-racing began around the turn of the century, there was no motor-racing World Championship as such until 1950. That was when somebody decided that the best performances across the Grands Prix of six European countries – plus, bizarrely, the Indianapolis 500 – should earn the title of World Champion.

At first, apart from the American race (which was run to different rules and almost totally ignored), every race was completely dominated by the Italian cars – Alfa Romeo, Ferrari and Maserati. The much-vaunted British contender, the V16 BRM, supported by British industry and donations from members of the public, was an abject and embarrassing failure. The champions were men like Farina, Ascari and – five times – Fangio, while the few British drivers tended to be wealthy amateurs with outmoded machinery. Then a debonair, blond young man called Mike Hawthorn, who always raced wearing a bow tie, was given a works Ferrari drive – and beat Fangio to win the 1953 French Grand Prix.

Meanwhile Stirling Moss, arguably the greatest, and surely the most versatile, driver Britain has ever produced, was determined to conquer the red cars and win for Britain in

British machinery. But as no British car existed that could do his bidding, he was forced to buy a Maserati and paint it green.

Meanwhile, if Britain couldn't shine in Formula 1, it was beating the world at sports car racing, and particularly in the most prestigious sports car race of all, the Le Mans 24 Hours. During the 1950s Jaguar beat Ferrari, Mercedes and the rest to win at Le Mans five times in seven years, and each time they did so all of Britain celebrated – because they'd been able to follow the race through the night, thanks to BBC Radio's regular reports. Incarcerated in a traditional boarding school, I invited terrible punishment by smuggling my portable radio into the dormitory so that I could listen under the blankets and be kept up to date by Baxter & Co.

Three times Moss was runner-up in the World Championship to Fangio: in 1955, driving for Mercedes Benz; in 1956, for Maserati; and in 1957, driving at last a dark green British contender, the Vanwall. Hawthorn and the dashing Peter Collins scored victories for Ferrari, and in 1958 the consistent Hawthorn beat the unlucky Moss by one point to become Britain's first World Champion. But the celebrations were clouded with tragedy: Collins had died at the Nurburgring, and within months a road accident took Hawthorn's life.

Nevertheless, by now the nascent British motor-racing industry was coming to life in little garages in south and north London, as first Cooper and then Lotus produced lightweight rear-engined cars that could outhandle and outrace the traditional machinery of Italy. And for us enthusiasts at home, with coverage in the papers still very scant, BBC Radio was usually the best source of news from the foreign races.

Coopers driven by an Australian, Jack Brabham, won the 1959 and 1960 titles. Ferrari fought back in 1961, but by 1962 Grand Prix racing had become virtually a British preserve. Every car on the grid but for the works Ferraris and Porsches was British. And, although Stirling Moss' career was over after a near-fatal crash at Goodwood, the top ten finishers in the World Championship all spoke English as their first language – four British, a New Zealander, an Australian, a South African and three Americans.

through no fault of his own was hard to bear. And in 1982 the unique and irreplaceable Gilles Villeneuve, the bravest and most spectacular of them all, was killed during qualifying for the Belgian Grand Prix at Zolder. His son Jacques was 11 at the time: 14 years later I was to describe his astonishing F1 debut in Australia, when he qualified first and finished second.

But the worst weekend of all was at Imola in 1994 for the San Marino Grand Prix. In Saturday qualifying the young Austrian Roland Ratzenburger was killed when his Simtek hit the barriers. It was the first fatal accident at a Grand Prix for 12 years, and it affected everyone deeply, not least triple World Champion Ayrton Senna, the brightest star in the motor-racing firmament, who even considered withdrawing from the next day's race. Then, 24 hours later, came Senna's still-unexplained accident at the Tamburello Corner.

From my commentary box I could see nothing of the crash, only the heart-wrenching pictures from Italian television on my monitor. Time stood still as the race was stopped and Professor Watkins and his medical team tended to the dying driver in the wreckage, and that was the scene I had to describe for the radio audience: that, and Ayrton's extraordinary career up to that point, and the lasting impression he had made on me as a very unusual man. Inevitably, information about the driver's condition was virtually non-existent, although I knew I had to expect the worst. It was several hours before an official announcement obliged me to confirm publicly what I already knew: that the greatest driver of his age was dead.

The saddest impressions remain, but so do the happiest ones, and none more than memories of darkness falling over the Suzuka circuit in Japan in October 1996. Several hours after Damon Hill had achieved his life's ambition and was champion at last, I was squashed into a tiny cabin behind the Williams pit, where he was celebrating with his friends. It seemed a very long time since I'd interviewed a youthful Formula Ford driver at Brands Hatch whose main claim to fame had been that his father had once been World Champion, or since I'd persuaded him to try his hand at radio and join me in the commentary box to describe a Silverstone Formula 3 race.

That evening he'd had enough of interviews, but in the press of people I was able to get for Five Live his wife Georgie's quiet thoughts on Damon's 15-year struggle up the motor-racing ladder, and the decent, honourable and very determined man she'd married. The tape of that, along with one of a chat I had in a hotel room with Niki Lauda, and another of a morning spent with Ayrton Senna during his first F1 season, I keep safely filed away. From time to time I play them again, to remind myself of the remarkable band of driven men I've been lucky enough to know, watch and describe on the radio over two decades.

RENTON LAIDLAW

The Pioneering Days of Golf on Radio

The long-serving Golf Correspondent of the
London Evening Standard, Renton Laidlaw
presented Sports Report *for two years. He is a*
devoted fan of Hibernian FC, a world authority
on airline timetables and a frustrated thespian.

With so much happening at so many places around the course, golf has never been an easy sport to cover especially if the scoring system is less than reliable. In the early days of radio broadcasting, Army territorials using, as best they could, antiquated field telephones were charged with the task of passing information back to the press centre. Even if the 'phones worked and the soldiers, always keen as mustard to do the job well, managed to make contact with us, there never was any guarantee that the figures or the facts were totally accurate. 'You mean they both had albatross 2's at the fifth ... hello ... can you repeat please ... did you say 2's ... he's gone' was how the conversation might go between the controller, usually a young officer, and the squaddie with the radio.

It was hardly surprising therefore that radio coverage of golf tournaments 40 years ago was most likely to be an end-of-the-day summary of scores which the reporter, Tom Scott in England and Peter Thomson in Scotland, knew to be correct. It was called limiting the damage, but even then there were pitfalls. Thomson, the legendary Glasgow-based BBC sports editor, would embark enthusiastically on a ten-minute sequence of results from the Scottish Amateur Championship – in the days when amateur golf carried more importance than it does today – which left the listener in an hypnotic trance. A beat B, C lost to D, E lost to F, G beat H ... a relentless litany made more interesting later by the fact that he enlisted the help of 'another voice' to help him wade through them. By the end you sometimes could not work out who had beaten or who had lost to whom, but it was a service and the sporting public were grateful for any news.

At least Peter never got himself so confused that he was faded out – the humiliation that was experienced by one young Scottish broadcaster who got himself in such a fankle reading the fishing news that BBC Scotland had to revert to emergency plan 'A' – mixing from the unintelligibly read fishing data for anxious trawlermen out in the Atlantic or North Sea wondering which port to head for to get the best prices, for the calmer but less informative strains of Jimmy Shand and his Band playing his own arrangement of the 'Dashing White Sergeant'. They never let that reporter loose on golf, thank goodness. Indeed he quickly moved to a more comfortable role well away from any microphone.

John Fenton, who had learned his broadcasting crafts in BBC Radio's Light Entertainment Department in the days of Ted Ray and Peter Brough and Archie Andrews, and as producer of the *Show Band Show* featuring Cyril Stapleton and his Orchestra, was one of the prime movers in the coverage of golf on radio, achieving something almost as remarkable as that managed by Peter Brough. Brough made his money as a ventriloquist on radio – not, you might think, all that demanding, although when he later moved to television listeners-turned-viewers could see how good he was at throwing his voice without making his lips move. John Fenton's Brough-like *coup de grâce* was to convince John Jacobs, the Yorkshire professional who was known as Dr Golf in the days before he masterminded the formation of the PGA European Tour, to do an instructional series on radio without even the help of diagrams in *Radio Times*. It is a tribute to Fenton's ingenuity as a producer and to the desire by radio's golf-minded listeners to improve their games that the improbable series was a huge success.

As a teenager, John Fenton first joined the old BBC as a trainee engineer with career prospects as sure and sound (if you will excuse the pun) in those days as those of pupils who left school to join a bank or an insurance office. How things have changed! The BBC in those days was a job for life, and London seemed populated by people who had worked at some stage for 'Auntie', were working for the BBC or hoped to work for the Corporation. In broadcasting terms it was considered that you had not been properly trained if you had not spent some time at Broadcasting House or Crystal Palace. John became radio's golf producer at a time when European golf was beginning to boom, although far less air time was available to him than Tony Adamson and his team enjoy today on Radio 5 Live. Not that the battle to get air time for golf worried Mr Fenton. To him getting the golf reports on was a wonderful challenge, and as Seve Ballesteros, Nick Faldo, Ian Woosnam, Sandy Lyle and Bernhard Langer began to take over on the international scene from Tony Jacklin and Peter Oosterhuis it became easier for him to convince producers that golf was worth more than a cursory read on a sports bulletin. Fortunately Bob Burrows, sports editor at the time, needed no convincing that the one thing British golfers were doing was winning titles and cups, and in British and Irish terms that was always worth shouting from the rooftops.

Compared with the sophistication of today's broadcasts (the BBC Radio team at the 1997 Open consisted of 16 people – reporters, editors, producers, engineers), John was often a one-man band operating not with pencil-slim radio mikes and digital state-of-the-art editing facilities but with cumbersome recording equipment and the old fashioned telephone which did not always work effectively. Back in the late 1960s it was not possible to direct dial as easily as we do now. When abroad John or I would have to make contact with Broadcasting House through the international operator, which was a stressful operation if you were in Spain, as we both found out to our cost.

Covering the Madrid Open, which was originally staged on three courses, had always been a bit of a nightmare. The pressroom used to be set up in a city-centre hotel, and reports of what had been happening were funnelled through to the part-time press officer, a charming lady who, because she was studying to be a lawyer, brought all her books with her to pore over during the long periods of inactivity. When her 'phone rang it was almost an inconvenience and the news received was sketchy. 'Tito Abreu was five under par when he had to withdraw at the 11th,' she would say. 'Why?' we would ask. 'Because he was playing well! 'No, why did he leave the course? Was he hit by a ball, disqualified, taken ill?' 'Don't know!' It was organised frustration.

Later, when the event became a one-course tournament and a press centre was established in a room on the first floor of the Puerto de Hierro clubhouse, the problem was not obtaining the information but getting it through to London. Communicating was a nightmare at every level. Because the course was built on a hill communicating from the course to the clubhouse was almost impossible. There was no radio link, as now, between the recorder's hut and the press room. Official scorecards were passed up to the first-floor pressroom by using a basket on a pulley. Cards were placed in the basket; an official gave a shout and a tug on the rope and anyone in the pressroom pulled the basket up. Having got the scores, getting through to your newspaper or the BBC involved another lengthy process. In short it was a nightmare. You gave your number to the non-English speaking club telephonist who did her best to contact the seemingly always intransigent international exchange operator in Paris whose job it was to connect you to London if she could be bothered.

Once contact had been made the farce was hardly over. Calls could only be received in one of four bedrooms situated on the second floor of the clubhouse. The system was primitive to say the least. Having booked the call you retreated some 50 yards along a narrow corridor to the foot of the stairs to await the telephone girl's less than cheerful shout that you were through. At that moment a phone would ring in one of the bedrooms. But which one? Inevitably the first one you went into was not the one she had rung so you quickly put the receiver back on its cradle and dashed to the next bedroom, but as you lunged to pick up the 'phone it stopped ringing. The operator, thinking you were not there, had switched the call to the room you had first gone into ... and this crazy version of pass-the-parcel or musical chairs usually ended with you having to dash back to the switchboard to ask the girl to try to connect you again. If John or I ever did get through we had a legitimate excuse for being slightly breathless – but the whole operation kept you fit.

With a threatened boycott of the tournament by pressmen because of the communication difficulties, officials alerted us that things would be different in future because a new direct-dial telephone exchange was being built. The following year as we drove to the course we passed a burned out building. 'What happened there? I queried. 'Oh, that was the new telephone exchange. It was burned to the ground,' said the courtesy car driver. The Madrid Open is no longer staged but, to be frank, I miss the excitement and the golf was good too.

Early radio reporting of golf on the Continent was always a hit-or-miss affair. Unaware or even worse unwilling to make themselves cogniscent of the problems the golf reporter was experiencing in the field, young producers, operating from their air-conditioned offices in London, sometimes let us down. Having promised to ring back at a certain time they would not do so. The consequence of this was that, rather like planes leaving Heathrow that are delayed, they lost their slot because there was only one telephone available for the whole press corps. If the call should have been made at 2.00 but was not tried until 2.10 it was impossible to get through. The line was being used by someone else. Once at a venue just outside Madrid a sophisticated arrangement of call-times was drawn up to give everyone the chance of catching their editions or making their radio deadlines. This was thrown innocently into total confusion when seconds before the first call was about to be made the local butcher 'phoned in to ask the club steward what his meat order was for the following week. From that moment on nobody got their call on time.

In the early days of reporting The Masters it was not much better. In those days the pressroom, now one of the most modern media centres in golf, was a converted Nissen hut – a structure with a semi-circular corrugated steel roof which was not in the least soundproof from any heavy shower. Since the press were crowded in like sardines it was almost impossible to broadcast with any real confidence. In the circumstances John Fenton had a brainwave. He befriended the greenkeeper who had a 'phone in his plush office just a few yards away from the press centre. From there John could contact Radio 2 or BBC World Service, operating in those palmy days from Bush House at the bottom of Kingsway, in the sure knowledge that the quality of the line would be such that he could be heard at the other end. The greenkeeper was delighted to help until the Masters officials found out and put a stop to it. Instantly Fenton was back in the noisy media tent shouting his reports down a crackly line.

Conditions for broadcasting in some foreign media tents, including the US Open press centre, were so bad acoustically that at times I was forced to construct my own radio studio out of a cardboard box. Passing my apparently empty desk other reporters might have been surprised to hear a muffled voice coming from somewhere – but where? In order to get reasonable-quality acoustics I was broadcasting from under the desk with a cardboard box placed over my head. The late-lamented Peter Dobereiner, hearing me speak in one broadcast about the bad weather and heavy rain, drummed his fingers on the top of the box, simultaneously whispering in my ear, 'This is the rain.' Ad-libbing furiously I told listeners, 'You can probably hear how heavy it is.'

John Fenton pioneered the use of on-course radios to bring instant news of the leaders to listeners, although this did not always work as effectively as it should have. Sometimes the trees affected the signals as John, a heavy radio transmitter strapped to his bag and an aerial protruding, it seemed, from his left ear, trudged round attempting to keep up with the play but stay far enough back to ensure his reports did not put a player off. There is, after all, nothing worse for a player about to line up a tricky downhill left to righter on a slick green, than to hear the on-course reporter saying, 'If he holes this one he'll be lucky!' John was always very careful about that and long before George Bayley became known as 'Whispering George' John had perfected the art of whispering into the microphones so effectively that his voice emerged on full power at the other end.

For many years we operated together in the commentary box, often perched on the top of a rickety scaffolding behind the green. The scaffolders knew the construction would not collapse, but we didn't as we struggled up the swaying ladder clutching our briefcases in one hand and knowing full well that we were not covered by any BBC insurance if we fell. It was down the same ladders that John would make his faster-than-light exits at the end of the programme. I would be closing up and turn to John for a final comment, only to see that he had already packed up his stopwatch and was so far down the ladder that only his head was still visible as he rushed to drive his orange Volkswagen known as the 'Carrot' out of the car park before anyone else. By the time the presentation was being staged John Fenton was 20 miles down the road and well clear of the area.

Sometimes the commentary boxes were not placed correctly. In the days before Gordon Turnbull, whose father Alex ran BBC World Service Sport for many years, took over production and ensured that they were, John and I found that, while we were always able to see the last green, we could not always see the huge scoreboard – vital in the days before MSL and Unisys had perfected a computerised system that makes Tony Adamson's job easy. In the old days you had to be good at mental arithmetic to ensure that the scores broadcast were correct. Once at The Belfry, the headquarters of the PGA, there was a major mishap in that no commentary position had been provided. In the end we worked from a room in the hotel – the window of which was at right angles to the scoreboard. When giving the leader boards we had to lean half out of the window, twist round and hope that we got through the top ten before falling into the flower beds below. The listeners never knew the difficulties under which we were operating.

Golf outside broadcasts, made more easy by the sterling work of engineer Ken Keen, improved so much over the years that eventually we were able to produce the Saturday afternoon show wholly from the golf event. It meant highly sophisticated communications in order to co-ordinate the golfing outside broadcast with all the other sporting OBs included in the six-and-a-half-hour show. Imagine our surprise when, within a few minutes of the complicated programme going on air at Royal St George's in 1985, the year that Sandy Lyle won the Open, there was a commotion and our commentary position was overrun by the Board of Governors led by the Director-General himself. The latter dignitary may never have been so rudely treated. As the countdown to the programme began I gave the deputation a cursory welcome. simultaneously asking them to be quiet. Unwisely one of the governors tapped Fenton, concentrating at the time on mastering the mechanics of his very basic scoring computer, on the shoulder as a prelude to asking him a question. John jumped round like a startled rabbit and gave the well-dressed culprit the hard stare. The governors quickly retreated when the sound of the *Sport on Two* (now *Sport on Five* signature tune) – 'No. 1' by the Delle Haensch Band from the album *Rhythm and Sport* – broke the awkward silence. We went on air. They went out the door.

To my eternal shame I was involved in one incident during another tournament at Royal St George's that is still talked about. So interested was I in making sure that the scores were correct that after Nick Faldo had holed out to win the event, I told the listeners that Sandy Lyle, with whom he had played the final round, was the winner. I realised my mistake instantly, and in order to make sure everyone knew who the real winner was I did everything but spell the name Faldo out. Some people who were listening that afternoon are convinced I did say: 'So Faldo – that is F-A-L-D-O – is the winner.' I kept my job and lived to make several more mistakes before passing the baton over to Tony Adamson. On another occasion I had had a reasonably fraught afternoon at the World Match-play.

Coming to the end of the semi-finals on the Saturday at around 4.45 I knew what had to be done – a quick resume of the situation, then switch to Don Mosey on the course for a further explanation of one semi-final, back to me for a tight link into Chris Rae's expert summary of the other semi-final, and then a final round up from me – all to be done in three minutes 15 seconds.

Just before I was about to start, producer Turnbull shouted into my ear, 'Go to Rae first, wrap up the other match, ask Don about an incident at the 15th, and then lead after two minutes 30 seconds to the cricket scoreboard.' For some reason I only half took it in and suddenly I was on … I started but I was sure that, unlike Magnus Magnusson, I wouldn't be able to finish because my mind had gone blank. I could not remember the sequence. I continued to talk but I was sure it was gibberish when suddenly, as if snapped out of a mini-coma, I came to and got on track. Afterwards I telephoned London to excuse myself for the inadequacy of the lead-in to the golf. Before I could launch into my apology, however, the overall programme producer said, 'Great stuff … thanks Renton, back to you in 30 minutes.'

Sometimes our reports had to be put on tape. Skilled editors, using their razor blades as expertly as a surgeon uses his knife to cut the audio tape, put together wonderful compilations which accurately summarised the day's play linked by suitable words from me. You can imagine the confusion one afternoon when we discovered 30 seconds before it was time to play out the tape that the editor had inadvertently put the required tape in the bucket and put the discarded bits on the machine! Somehow – and I still do not know how – the real tape was on the machine and ready to be played a split second before I started the report.

Live radio has always been invigorating but never more so than at that Open at St Andrews when I was hosting a half-hour programme for BBC Scotland from a small caravan parked just outside the famous R and A clubhouse. One half of the caravan was filled with the broadcasting equipment, the engineer and the producer. The other half had the microphone, a table, me, two reporters to talk about specific performances that afternoon, an American who was to compare British golf events with American tournaments, two players who were to discuss the difficulties of certain holes and I think an official from the R and A. The caravan was so small that some of the personnel were lying on the floor and I had to pass the microphone down to them to do their sections. The real problem was that internal communications had broken down and the producer was unable to communicate to me. I needed to know when to start certain sections so we devised an elaborate system whereby the producer held aloft a white handkerchief and dropped it when I had to start. It all worked until half-way through the programme another contributor arrived to say his piece. Unable to get into the caravan, the door of which had been locked to seal us all in, he started knocking on the windows causing the studio to rock on its wheels. The producer, still clutching the white handkerchief, fell over but we completed the programme and came out on time – always a prerequisite.

Those were the days, but at least today the coverage is so sophisticated that it makes you laugh to think what had to be done in the past to bring listeners the latest golfing news. The Old course at St Andrews is one which goes all the way out to the turn and then all the way back. Reporters used to ride out to the ninth and back on rented bicycles to get half-way scores. On one occasion with deadlines approaching a plan was devised by one astute journalist that, in the event of the leader holing a birdie putt, the reporter's colleague, walking with the game, would raise and open his umbrella. The fellow back at base would train his RAF binoculars on the moving crowd and be able to advise others in the media tent what had happened, but the plan went horribly wrong. Just as the players were disappearing into the far distance, the rain came on and umbrellas went up all over the place. Now all we have to worry about is a power-cut making all our computers go down.

What is certain is that covering golf for BBC Radio remains one of the most enjoyable jobs in sport. Just to have been there and told the world that Jack Nicklaus or Seve Ballesteros or

Nick Faldo has won the Open at St Andrews, that Sam Torrance has holed the winning putt in the 1985 Ryder Cup at The Belfry, or that we have won the Cup for the first time on American soil two years later, gave me a thrill. To have reported a Walker Cup victory in 1989 at Peachtree in Atlanta, or that terrific duel between Jack Nicklaus and Tom Watson at Turnberry in 1977, or the first golf Open in China, or that dramatic Sandy Lyle success at Augusta, was, truly, to have been in a privileged position.

MAGIC MOMENTS...

Sometimes broadcasters can tempt fate and bring misfortune on themselves. Broadcast lines from football grounds have a habit of misbehaving, but while he was commentating on one of Celtic's European ties from Parkhead Peter Drury's broadcast equipment chose precisely the wrong moment to 'explode'.

Peter's commentary went something like this: 'I'm a fairly optimistic chap, but even I'm struggling with this one. Celtic 3-nil down on the night, so they need to score five in the last 20 minutes. All I can say is that if they win from here, you're about to hear the most exciting –' CIRCUIT EXPLODES.

BILL McLAREN

Rugby Union's World Cup

*The voice of Rugby Union on BBC Television for
more than 40 years, Bill McLaren has covered all
three World Cup competitions, the last two for
BBC Radio. A proud native of Hawick in the
Scottish Borders, Bill is never without his tin of
Hawick Balls (boiled sweets!) to sustain him in
the commentary box.*

Ever since their visit to my home town, Hawick, in the Scottish
Border country all those years ago in 1935, I have held the All
Blacks in some awe. On that occasion they played the South of
Scotland, and I vividly recall sitting in the enclosure seat as a 12-
year-old schoolboy and seeing the New Zealand captain, Jack
Manchester, *walk* his team on to the field like large, black
prophets of doom. To my jaundiced gaze they seemed to exude
menace and each one seemed to have the physical attributes of
King Kong!

Since that day I have had vast admiration and respect for
New Zealand Rugby men whose total commitment to the cause
of winning Rugby was forcibly brought home to me in the first
of the World Cup tournaments held in Australia and New
Zealand in 1987. It was just before the final in that tournament
in which New Zealand were to meet France at Eden Park,
Auckland, that I attended the final New Zealand training
session. It took my breath away. On one pitch John Hart, that
master coach and tactician, had the New Zealand backs eating

out of his hand as he guided them through refinements to their attack and defence alignments with methodical care. On an adjoining area the All Blacks forwards practised scrummaging until it was, as they say, 'coming out of their ears'.

I had never seen anything like that scrummaging session. I just boggled in amazement. Only seven months previously the French had shocked the Rugby world and most of all the All Blacks by beating them by 16–3 in Nantes. That French triumph had its foundation in a grinding French scrummage that caught the All Blacks unawares and that gave the French a more productive platform. All Blacks don't take kindly to playing second fiddle! They made up their minds that they would lay the ghost of that humiliation and, to that end, they staged the most physically demanding sessions of scrummaging that I had ever seen. For an hour, two eight-man packs battered into each other as perspiration cascaded all over the place. Brian Lochore, their renowned coach, was in charge and there was no letting up. You would have thought that the rival packs simply hated each other. It was almost frightening in its intensity and there were stoppages for bumps and bruises but no one wanted to give an inch. It did the trick. Those All Blacks were intent on ensuring that their scrummage would not be put at a disadvantage in the World Cup Final. It wasn't. Their scrummage became a strongpoint and that demonstrated just how quickly All Blacks learnt and how focused they are towards putting things to rights.

Actually that World Cup Final was a disappointment as a spectacle. The New Zealanders pinned the faith in their forwards and in the Grant Fox boot for a shoal of up-and-unders and positional punts. There can be no more daunting experience for a fullback than to be looking skywards at a descending mortar bomb with the sound of heavy New Zealand hoofbeats in his ears! Yet Serge Blanco, that prince of fullbacks, survived but shared in French disappointment in defeat by 29–9.

There were those who doubted the value of a World Cup competition as creating a form of win-at-all-costs Rugby in such a highly competitive environment that would be at odds with the sporting ethos of the amateur age. Yet the interest generated was mirrored in attendance figures – 355,500 at 21 games in New Zealand and 126,000 at 11 games in Australia. The competition was seen as providing a huge stimulus for the established nations while also giving a vehicle by which the emerging nations might measure their progress. Indeed such nations as Zimbabwe, Italy, Fiji, Japan and Canada did demonstrate, even in defeat, that the Rugby game did not belong to any group of countries but to the whole world.

The World Cup also presented a wonderful stage upon which outstanding personalities might strut their stuff. Michael Jones, the All Blacks flanker, whose religious beliefs precluded him from playing on Sundays, was described by one New Zealand media man as 'having the hands of a centre, the style of an athlete and tackling like a ton of bricks'. The New Zealand fullback John Gallagher scored four tries against Fiji in the pool game – four tries by a fullback. Extraordinary! The inimitable Serge Blanco scored the dramatic try that gave France semi-final victory over Australia by 30–24, a match in which the lead changed six times and which was described by that much respected Rugby correspondent, the late Clem Thomas, as 'one of the greatest Rugby games I have ever seen'. It was following that French win that their coach, Jacques Fouroux, known as *le petit général* said: 'And to think that we have been told that we are only kings in our own garden, the northern hemisphere! A false jibe.' There was, too, David Campese of Australia, then only 23 and playing fullback yet with 24 international tries (his current tally is 64) and demonstrating once again that outrageous individualism that has marked him out as the most entertaining player the game has spawned.

One has fond recall of providing BBC TV commentary when Greg Oliver, a former pupil, scored a debut try for Scotland against Zimbabwe, and not so fond recall of the monitor packing up during the Wales v Tonga pool match when so many of the Tongans looked alike!

So the World Cup was launched in some style. The games were beamed on television to 80 countries, 222 tries were scored in 32 games, there was high drama, tight tension, and some superb attacking Rugby. The spirit on the field was generally of a high order so that expectations were equally high when the second tournament was staged in England, Scotland, Ireland, Wales and France in 1991. It was hoped too that the game would be popularised as, for instance, in Australia where there had been a 15 per cent 'uptake' of youngsters in Rugby Union in the four years leading to the second event.

The 1991 World Cup provided a revealing insight into the workings of Radio Five sport and of the workload taken on by presenters and commentators to satisfy the voracious demands of that and other programmes. There was I on the opening day of the tournament, being hustled by *Obergruppenfuhrer* Charles Runcie into presenting myself at Twickenham at 7.30 am in order to contribute to two different programmes. About midday I found myself standing behind Twickenham's West stand doing a bit into a children's programme! It was all very hectic and I wondered what I had let myself in for. Indeed the commentary was the easy bit! Thanks to the guidance, organisation and friendship of Charles Runcie and the infectious enthusiasm of Ian Robertson (the only Scottish stand-off ever to have scored a try and dropped a goal in the first half against Wales at Cardiff Arms Park), one managed to keep head above water.

Perhaps the abiding memory was of how England changed their style for the final against Australia. They had held, in the main, to a restricted strategy on a narrow front especially in their 9–6 semi-final win over Scotland at Murrayfield when there wasn't a single try and the winning points came from a typical Rob Andrew drop goal. Geoff Cooke, England's coach, was quoted afterwards: 'We would love to have cut Scotland to pieces with scintillating back play but it is not quite as easy as that.' In any event the game did provide a milestone for two famous stalwarts. John Jeffrey led on the Scotland team to mark his last international appearance at Murrayfield, and Rory Underwood led on England as the first England player to reach 50 caps.

In the final, however, England ran the ball a lot more than

expected. Perhaps because they had not done so consistently in previous games, or because they thus departed from their established style or simply because the Australian defence was so organised and committed, they were unable to stitch together one try-scoring move and the Wallabies won by 12–6. In fact the only try highlighted the kind of situation that is something of a nightmare for radio and TV commentators. Willie Ofahengaue, the Tongan pile-driver won lineout ball and a mass of bodies drove over the England line. It was impossible to tell who had scored as both Tony Daly and Ewan McKenzie were congratulated by their colleagues. Eventually it was agreed that Daly had got the try!

Perhaps the most popular of all were the Western Samoans who might have caused pronunciation problems for Radio 5 and TV commentators with names such as Aiolupo, Fatialofa, Toomalatai, Alaalatoa and Tagaloa but who endeared themselves to the Murrayfield audience with their lap of honour to thank them for their sporting support after the 28–6 defeat by Scotland. Those Pacific islanders may have made some 'big hits' that bordered on the dangerous but they truly reflected the spirit of the Cup.

There was controversy. In the final, David Campese was deemed to have deliberately knocked on when faced with a two to one and a likely England try. Welsh referee Derek Bevan awarded a penalty to England that Jonathan Webb slotted to cut the Australian lead to 12–6. There was a body of opinion that a penalty try should have been awarded to England: that, with a conversion from in front of the posts, would have cut the deficit to just two points. I thought the referee was right. When a player is faced with a two to one near his own line there isn't much else he can do but stick out his arm and hope to prevent the ball reaching the overlap player. He might knock on in the process but that isn't generally the intention. The Australians, however, won the Webb Ellis trophy and their popular captain, Nick Farr-Jones, said afterwards: 'Everything you ever have done in Rugby becomes worthwhile when you win the World Cup.' He and his squad received a ticker tape welcome when they arrived home.

Now thoroughly well established, the third World Cup was staged very efficiently in South Africa in 1995, and not even their scriptwriters could have created a more dramatic final than that between South Africa and New Zealand, the acknowledged heavyweights of the world game.

The All Blacks laid before their entranced support a brand of Rugby that had 'modern' and 'entertainment' written all over it. They were superb at keeping the ball and at putting together long periods of continuous action that were breath-taking in their skill levels, speed and wondrous interplay under pressure. Yet they lost the final to a drop goal by Joel Stransky in the second minute of the second half of extra time that gave South Africa a 15–12 victory, Stransky scoring all their points with four penalty goals and a drop goal and Andrew Mehrtens all for New Zealand with three penalty goals and a drop goal. Not a try was scored but it was a riveting confrontation on a day when Nelson Mandela took much of the honour. There he was, wearing the number 6 Springbok jersey celebrating the South African victory with the actual number 6 François Pienaar, the South African captain. The president got it just right and his support for the Springboks inspired a unity within the ranks of all South Africans that was a delight to experience. New Zealand's famous manager, Brian Lochore, said to me that when he toured South Africa as a player in the All Blacks squad they knew that vast numbers of black South Africans supported the All Blacks. 'But this time round,' he said, 'we know that we are taking on the whole of South Africa.' Clearly the Rainbow Nation had come together in a celebration of new-found freedom.

Final day was some experience. A Boeing 747 reared overhead 50 feet above the stands bearing the message 'Good Luck Bokke'. The former mine dump and brickworks that has become the magnificent Ellis Park Stadium in Johannesburg echoed to euphoric acclaim by the close-on 63,000 crowd as François Pienaar made the point: 'We did not just have 63,000 cheering us on out there but 43 million.'

That 1995 World Cup launched on to the world stage the All Black Jonah Lomu who rapidly became the best-known Rugby player in the world. I first saw him when he was just 19 at a practice session by the New Zealand squad prior to the 1994 Hong Kong sevens. I recall asking Merrill Shannon, their manager, who the big forward was. 'You won't believe this, Bill, he isn't a forward, he's a bloody wing,' he chuckled. That took me aback because the lad was built like a grain store at 6 feet 5 inches and 18 stone 6 lb. I'd never seen a wing as big. Of course in sevens he was devastating but equally so in the fuller version as England discovered in the World Cup semi-final when Lomu ran in, or perhaps it should be 'thundered in', for four of New Zealand's six tries in their victory by 45–29. Lomu had arrived! Just how big he was can be gauged from the occasion when I entered a lift in the New Zealand party's hotel. Lomu was the only one in it, and I could hardly get in!

That World Cup tournament in South Africa also laid before an astonished audience three world records as New Zealand beat Japan by 145–17, Marc Ellis recorded six of their 21 tries, and a slim lad from Invercargill, Simon Culhane, scored 45 points from one try and 20 conversions! That evidence of the gulf that yet exists between the heavy artillery and the weaker brethren makes it questionable whether it is wise to have an increase in the number of teams for the fourth World Cup in Cardiff in 1999.

One other incident stands out. C. Runcie Esq. arranged for me to interview Laurie Mains, the New Zealand coach, for Radio Five Live. I was told that it would be a difficult interview as Mains tended to be a dour fellow and not very forthcoming. In fact he was a delight, articulate, forthright and thoroughly interesting. He actually made me look like a good interviewer, which takes a lot of doing! Nor did he dodge any question. Which goes to show that you should always judge folk as you find them and not as someone else finds them.

In any event the World Cup is now firmly established and eagerly awaited as always producing deserving World Champions. You cannot get any better surely than New Zealand, Australia and South Africa. Perhaps, however, the northern hemisphere will have its day in Cardiff in 1999. That would make the bells ring all right – and about time too!

JONATHAN AGNEW

Cricket in the 1990s: Shane Warne

The former Leicestershire and England fast bowler cut his teeth as a broadcaster in local radio and is now the BBC's Cricket Correspondent. 'Aggers' is a Sony Award winner and a prominent member of the Test Match Special team, where he has succeeded 'Johnners' as chief prankster.

There can have been few decades in the long and complicated history of Test cricket which have been so dramatic as the 1990s. The game has been subjected to just about every conceivable scandal from allegations of match fixing, ball tampering, bribery and, surely the most remarkable of all, the claim by a captain of Pakistan that a Test umpire had doctored the ball during a drinks break!

The steady breakdown in both discipline and the spirit of fair play required urgent action, so a code of conduct was introduced, complete with match referees to oversee it, and firm action was encouraged to stamp out intimidatory fast bowling and 'sledging'.

Its house finally put in order, South Africa was welcomed fully into the international fold for the first time. Calcutta hosted the opening match of the post-apartheid era, Mother Teresa gave the occasion her blessing and over 100,000 people packed Eden Gardens to watch India win a game which was dwarfed by the significance of it all. Sadly, even that moment of history was spoiled by further accusations of ball-tampering.

So it is with huge relief that cricket-lovers have relished the emergence of two truly great players who should, in time, mature to become cricketing giants. The names of Brian Lara, who broke the records for the highest Test score and the highest first-class score within seven weeks of one another, and Shane Warne, the prodigious Australian wrist spinner, already deserve to live alongside the very best in cricket's rich and colourful folklore.

However, while Lara set the world alight in 1994, it has been Warne who has made the greater overall impact. Remarkably, he has been able to keep his feet firmly on the ground despite his meteoric rise both in fame and income, and it was a joy to discover, as I interviewed Warne at the start of the 1997 Australian tour, that he was exactly the same amusing, likeable and relaxed man I had met for the first time four years earlier.

And who could ever forget his stunning introduction to Test cricket in England in 1993? Certainly not me, having been the one who had to commentate on his first delivery to Mike Gatting. I remember giving Warne, then aged only 23, quite a build-up as he prepared to bowl, only to have my view of the ball completely obscured both by Gatting's ample frame and Ian Healy, the wicket keeper who was standing up to the wicket.

It was only when Gatting, who had stood rooted to the spot while the Australian fielders danced in celebration all around him, finally began to trudge towards the pavilion with an occasional bewildered glance at the off bail which still lay on the ground, that the first slow motion was shown on television.

It was quickly called 'the ball from hell' and, for the life of me, I cannot imagine anyone playing it securely. It is all too easy to study the replays and criticise Gatting for not being a few more inches further forward. The fact was it was a loosener for bowler and batsman alike: neither had any right to expect that particular delivery to behave as it did.

The savage spin was only the final ingredient. Homing in towards Gatting's pads, the ball began to drift down the leg side until it was at least 18 inches wide of leg stump. At this stage, Gatting appeared to be content to allow it to spin back into his pads, only for the ball to rip out of the rough and hit the top of the off stump. Gatting was so mortified, he momentarily suspected that Healy might have knocked off the bail with his wicket-keeping gloves.

Warne's success is founded on three vital assets: his physical strength, his accuracy and his voracious appetite to learn new tricks. His shoulder and spinning fingers, which have been a source of concern through wear and tear, are massively developed and, particularly when accompanied by a Monica Seles-style grunt, he spins the ball further than, possibly, anyone with a legitimate action has ever done on a dry pitch.

He preys on the area outside a right hand batsman's leg stump which has been roughened up by the bowler's footmarks. Sometimes Warne goes round the wicket to exploit it still further to make run-scoring almost impossible (which increases still further the pressure on the batsmen) and this has given rise to some extraordinary, almost freakish dismissals: Graham Gooch being bowled behind his legs at Edgbaston in 1993, for example. And, at Sydney in 1997, Shivnarine Chanderpaul was bowled by a massive legbreak which exploded from fully 2 feet outside the off stump and hit leg. They, along with Gatting's delivery, are all on a video tape which Warne carries in his bag at all times just in case, as in the early summer of 1997, his confidence takes a dip.

Wrist spinners instinctively get on well with one another – they speak the same confusing language, after all. Theirs is a world of googlies, flippers, boseys and chinamen, and Warne has found an especially close soul-mate in the brilliant Pakistani leg spinner, Abdul Qadir. They met during an Australian tour of the sub-continent and Warne returned to talk effusively about a couple of hours they had spent together at either end of a silk carpet, spinning a cricket ball to one another, developing and even inventing new skills. The result was the 'zooter', a Warne prototype which is unveiled periodically to baffle batsmen still further.

One effect is clear to see. There has, in the 1990s, been a mini-renaissance in the art of wrist-spin bowling, not just in Australia but here, too, on the village greens of England. And for that, we should all be thankful.

PATRICK COLLINS

A View from the Street

Sports columnist with the Mail on Sunday,
*Patrick Collins is an astute observer of the
sporting scene and a long-standing listener and
contributor to* Sports Report.

Several years have passed since that winter Saturday evening
when a BBC sports commentator took his seat in the dining-car
of a London-bound express. A few hours earlier he had covered
a match at Maine Road, and now he and his companions began
a vigorous discussion on the shortcomings of Manchester City.

The argument was scarcely under way when a steward
approached and offered the commentator a card. Without
looking up or breaking sentence, the BBC man continued to
detail City's inadequacies as he snatched the card, produced a
pen, and wrote: 'Yours in Sport, Best Wishes…'.

The steward appeared visibly stunned. 'I don't know who
you are, squire,' he said, 'but you've just scribbled all over
tonight's menu.'

As I said, it happened several years ago and the commentator
in question was not some outrageous poseur but a pleasant
man, briefly yielding to delusions of celebrity. Sadly, this did not
save him. You see, his dining companions were of the inky-
fingered, hold-the-back-page variety, and the anecdote giggled
its way through every pub in Fleet Street before the weekend
was through.

There was, in those days, an ill-defined but unmistakable line of demarcation. Real reporters carried notebooks, asked awkward questions, teased out stories and worked for newspapers. Other reporters carried microphones, criticised nobody, faithfully purveyed the thoughts of the Establishment and worked in radio or television. Why, in certain circumstances, you could almost imagine them signing autographs on dining-car menus.

Recently, I heard Mike Ingham, Alan Green and Charlotte Nicol cover a match in the Midlands. It was a poor game, marred by a certain amount of cynical violence, and the BBC trio did not spare it. Ingham's commentary, earlier in the afternoon, had been a model of lucid disapproval. Green's match verdict on *Sports Report* fairly sizzled with Ulster scorn, while Ms Nicol's post-match interviews for the programme were shrewd and pointed. It was authentic, hard-nosed, sharp-elbowed reporting. You could almost hear the celestial grunt of approval from Angus Mackay, the tough old Scottish producer who kicked the whole thing into life half a century ago.

Through each of its five decades, *Sports Report* has always been a touch more acerbic than most of the Corporation's sports programmes; a prickly oasis in a vast expanse of comfortable cordiality. Now there was a time when BBC cricket commentators served in the same regiments and belonged to the same clubs as the men who controlled affairs at Lord's, when BBC rugby men believed without question that Twickenham was the repository of all truth, honour and decency, and when certain BBC tennis commentators shared both the accents and attitudes of the crusty luminaries of the All-England Club.

Sports Report was different, although it took time to find its own distinctive tone. The first presenter, Raymond Glendenning, was a hugely celebrated and remarkably skilful broadcaster, yet to modern ears his voice was better suited to the coronation of a monarch than the confirmation of an offside decision. They were gentler, less assertive times, as indicated by Glendenning's opening words on 3 January 1948. 'Our aim is to bring into your home, wherever you may be, a half-hour coverage of sport, wherever it may be taking place.

How well we have succeeded in this first edition, you will be able to judge after the next twenty-nine minutes.' Only the script survives to tell us what Glendenning said, since no recording was made. But we see that there were no claims, no promises and not even a hint of chest-thumping bravado. 'We'll do our very best,' he was saying, 'and we hope it all works out. We really, really do.'

In truth, the jury was never in doubt. Post-war Britain was turning out at events in unprecedented numbers and demonstrating an insatiable appetite for all kinds of sport. The sporting nation was searching for the kind of coverage which would reflect its interests. Scarcely 100,000 families possessed a television, while newspapers were savagely restricted by the rationing of newsprint. So it just had to be radio and, very swiftly, it just had to be *Sports Report*.

Ten years ago, at the time of the fortieth anniversary, I suggested that Mackay, the first producer, was the man who invented Saturday tea-time: burning toast, nibbled finger nails and watching the newsprint soaking up the ink as you scribbled the football results in the columns of the morning papers. It wasn't the fact or even the substance of the programme. No, it was the tune which introduced it: 'Out of the Blue', from the peerless pen of Hubert Bath. *Dee-dum, dee-dum, dee-dum, dee-dum, dee diddley dum dee-daaah*! For those of us who still cherish a childishly romantic fascination for sport and sports people, that tune is the guarantee that something marvellous is about to happen.

Although radio was, in theory, a rival medium, some of the nation's finest sports writers played an honourable part in establishing the programme half a century ago. Along with the results and the reports, the dominating sound of those early days was the sound of argument; the kind of argument you might have heard in Fleet Street pubs. The public delighted in the Harrovian drawl of Peter Wilson, the languid ruminations of Geoffrey Green and the hectoring, incisive tones of J. L. Manning, all of them obeying with style and passion the central edict of their craft – that they should comfort the afflicted and afflict the comfortable. All three are gone, just as the men with whom they tussled are gone, Jack Solomons, Alan Hardaker, Stanley Rous, Jack Crump and the like. Those names may ring no bells with the present generation of sports followers, yet in their day their power to control sporting affairs seemed almost unlimited.

From time to time, it probably crossed the minds of Wilson, Green and Manning that they were being used to inject controversy into *Sports Report*, since BBC staff correspondents were expected to remain loftily unaligned. But if the writers realised, then certainly they didn't mind a bit. '*Sports Report* was like belonging to a rather good club,' Peter Wilson told me towards the end of his life. 'You turned up every Saturday and argued the toss with some very entertaining people. Splendid fun, it was. Such splendid fun that I was always amazed that they paid me to go on it. Not much, mind, but they paid me. D'you know, I'd have done it for nothing.'

In this television age, it seems scarcely credible that 12 million listeners would sit by their radios every Saturday evening to listen to Wilson and his chums arguing the toss. But the mixture of reporting and discussion was precisely what the nation had been seeking, and *Sports Report* quickly became not so much a programme but an institution in the making.

Year by year, decade by decade, the institution became sharper and less respectful. The old Fleet Street heavyweights yielded to the pressure of event-led coverage, but that coverage had acquired a more irreverent tone. If a match was turgid, then the reporters would list the shortcomings rather than scramble for excuses. Now this reality was partially obscured by the fact that most of the major correspondents sounded as if they had come tumbling out of the top drawer. Bryon Butler might easily have been the Honourable Member for Loamshire South, rising from the backbenches to make a mellifluous intervention in a debate on cattle prices. It was difficult to reconcile the reassuring rustic vowels with the frequently trenchant views – until you remembered that Butler had been reared in a hard school of urgent deadlines and forthright opinions.

The late Peter Jones was an equally plausible Establishment figure, slim, dapper and Cambridge-courteous. He once hauled me out of a mountain snow drift while covering the 1984 Winter Olympics in Sarajevo. He stifled his chuckles, dusted me down and produced a hip flask brimming with brandy. 'Could happen to anyone, old chap,' he said, with only a flickering hint of smugness. It was Jones who presented the fortieth anniversary edition of *Sports Report*, and he wore a dinner jacket in the studio to mark the occasion. 'What do you imagine you look like, Jonesy?' I inquired, remembering the smugness of Sarajevo. He simply swatted me. 'It's all about a little thing called "class", dear boy,' he smirked. 'Not sure you'd understand.'

Peter loved to pass himself off in a vaguely Woosterish light, but the act was never truly convincing. For some of us had heard him at Heysel, conveying the unthinkable and articulating the unspeakable. A reporter from the top drawer, was Peter Jones, hugely admired and sadly missed.

But if Jones, with his cut-glass vowels, vividly represented *Sports Report*, then so too does Jimmy Armfield, with his enormous reserves of experience and his almost childish delight in the national game. Jim comes from that part of Lancashire where English football was nurtured and where it is still most deeply respected. Armfield conveys that respect every time he picks up a microphone.

Inevitably, football dominates the hour of *Sports Report*, but the other significant sports are covered with splendid panache. Peter Bromley may have spent his afternoon yelling the horses home, yet still he is able to encapsulate odds, opinions and objective description in the merest fragment of air-time. Tony Adamson brings a beguiling touch of whimsy to the intensity of professional golf. And then there is John Rawling. Not content with being the most impressive commentator that track and field has known since David Coleman were a lad, Rawling has developed into a genuine authority on the sport they used to call The Noble Art. At a time when hype is king, mis-matches abound and gimmickry is valued more highly than talent, Rawling calls boxing as he sees it. And if his candour does not endear him to the sensitive philanthropists who control the sport, then so be it.

Of course the programme is imperfect. It is still afflicted by an endless line of players and managers who decorate every sentence with a 'hopefully' and a 'very much so'. Much more importantly, it still refuses to award Charlton Athletic the full and comprehensive coverage which that incomparable football club demands and deserves. But, those blemishes apart, the old girl is operating at the peak of her form as she enters her fiftieth year.

When I was searching for a few words to convey appreciation of the achievement, I came across this offering from radio reviewer and author Jeremy Clarke, writing in the *Sunday Telegraph*:

> Every Saturday afternoon at five o'clock, between now and next May, I will be joining those gathered in that great Victorian railway terminus of the nation's consciousness known as *Sports Report*, to hear James Alexander Gordon read the football results in the same measured and orderly manner that many of us first heard when we were in the womb. Has anybody ever heard this marvellous man say 'Heart of Midlothian nil, Hamilton Academical 1' without feeling that the world isn't such a bad place after all?

Ah, yes. 'That great Victorian railway terminus of the nation's consciousness'. And somewhere above the clatter of trolleys and the hissing of steam, I fancy I hear a very familiar tune: *Dee-dum, dee-dum, dee-dum, dee-dum, dee diddley dum dee-daaah!* Very Hubert Bath. Very *Sports Report*. Very much so.

PATRICK MURPHY

Hunting the Quarry

*Radio Sport's Man in the Midlands since 1981,
Patrick Murphy talks and writes about football
and cricket with equal alacrity. He is the presenter
of* Any Sporting Questions *and many feature series
and has written more than thirty books, including
biographies of Ian Botham and Brian Clough.*

I must have been a precociously horrid little sniveller, all those
years ago, as I listened to *Sports Report*, gathered round the
dinner table with my sports-mad family. I remember so vividly
those early years of the programme, as the warring factions of
our household settled tacitly on a truce as soon as the strains of
'Out of the Blue' boomed out of the wireless. What I don't
remember is a forecast I made at the age of five. Thirty years on,
I was reminded of it by my mother after I had my debut on
Sports Report in 1981. It appears that I had blithely announced
to my family, 'One day, I'm going to be reporting on that
programme' – the kind of arrogant statement that deserved the
sharp elbow in the ear technique beloved of Basil Fawlty
whenever a kid got uppity. Anyway, my mother filed that
moment away in the memory bank until I got there, and the
revelation produced a suitably sheepish blush from yours truly.
Yet, if you accept that some ambitions lurk beneath the surface
surprisingly early in life, I'm happy now to be reminded of that
brash forecast, made when Billy Wright was my hero and
Duncan Edwards was crunching into his tackles. For me,

contributing every week to *Sports Report* is my career highlight, an enduring privilege to grasp regularly a torch that's been handed down over the generations by so many illustrious performers.

It remains a stern professional challenge when you're one of the programme's football reporters, and it's getting harder, as precious minutes slip away between the final whistle and appearing live on the air. That period of time is shrinking, now that half-time has been extended to fifteen minutes and so much more is added on by the referee because players have feigned injury, looking for the penalty after falling to the ground as if the sniper in the stand is on a productivity bonus. Usually the game ends just a few minutes before five o'clock, and after dashing off a breathless live thirty seconds, you then settle down to write a considered piece to be broadcast live within the next ten or fifteen minutes. Then the producer comes on the talk-back after deciding that your match has been sufficiently important to warrant an interview with a player or manager. There's the rub, as they say on the Kop. If the game is that important, then you'll be on early with your report. So, as you wonder who the Sam Hill you can grab for a chat in the bowels of the stadium, a long way from your reporting post, you try to conjure up a telling phrase or two as the minutes race along. It's at times like these that the strains of 'Out of the Blue' down your headphones are about as welcome as a verruca to Naomi Campbell. 'Is it that time already?' you bellow frantically, as the Muse of journalistic inspiration stubbornly refuses to sit on your shoulder – 'I haven't written a bloody thing yet, and I'm on in five minutes!' You pray that James Alexander Gordon elongates his elegant reading of the results, you try to ignore the stentorian bellows of adjoining reporters on local radio stations, you vow to get a less stressful job in your declining years – and then, miraculously, you manage to sound like a tolerably sane human being when the name check comes from the presenter.

Not without the occasional blemish, though. My handwriting would spark pangs of jealousy from any doctor, and it's even worse on duty for *Sports Report*. How else could I explain the day when I informed the nation that a certain player deserves to add to his tally of 'just seven craps for England'?

So, as you rise from your seat in the press box, wondering why such seats are designed only for those under five feet, you gird your loins for the next *Sports Report* challenge. The post-match interview. Stalking the reluctant quarry, the player or manager who has been wound up all day like a cheap watch, and would now appreciate some time to calm down, thank you very much. Unfortunately, that is no longer an option in the current world of sports coverage, where banal quotes are worshipped unduly because they at least come from the horses mouths. So you negotiate the rapids around the changing room, trying to get near to the appropriate subject in the shortest space of time. Sadly, the *Sports Report* representative is not the only broadcaster with the same idea. The great god television is stalking the land as well, mob-handed, talking pompously into their walkie-talkies, informing their directors how near they are to landing their fish, with all the solemnity of a presidential bodyguard at an airport. All this means that the player takes even longer to get ready than normal, so that he can look his best for the cameras. Must have that baseball cap at a jaunty angle, with the sponsor's logo suitably prominent. In vain do you try to reach an accommodation with the television representatives over priority of programmes, pointing out that you need your player within five minutes or you've run out of time and your producer will be less than chuffed. There is even less point in underlining that they have annexed the radio interview positions that have been part of the dressing-room scene for years. If the television battalions see a spare room, that's theirs by squatters' rights, and the resulting interview is sometimes conducted live alongside the TV crew interrogating someone else. That doesn't make for an ideal ambience, as you try to get some sense out of a footballer who has pushed himself so hard mentally and physically up until half-an hour ago. Still, never mind – the game is now run for television's benefit, and the rest of us ought to be grateful for the privilege of seeing their crack regiments, working hand-to-hand at close quarters.

It wasn't always such a hassle. There have been many in the

football industry who respected the contribution of *Sports Report* and willingly fronted up at the shortest notice, conducting the interview in a quiet part of a corridor, or even the sauna or the physio's couch. Anywhere that's tolerably quiet. That's the beauty of radio – you can be in and out, on your own, inside three minutes, because *Sports Report* simply hasn't time for anything much longer. You're looking to finish your football coverage by 5.30, so that other sports can be featured before the racing results are read twenty minutes later, and the programme starts to wrap up. In the 1980s, one of the Saturdays that really got the pulse rate soaring was always F.A. Cup semi-final day. A convention evolved that we would get the two successful managers together from their respective grounds, linking them up with the studio presenter, for the ritual babble about the Twin Towers, the new Wembley suit and the prospect of playing next season in the European Cup-Winners' Cup. In 1983 Ron Atkinson's Manchester United won at Villa Park and, against the odds, Brighton triumphed over Sheffield Wednesday at Highbury. I was charged with the responsibility of getting Big Ron out of his euphoric dressing-room, and easing him into the headphones. Ron was, of course, an old hand at such matters and he was in good, wisecracking form as he waited to hear from his fellow Liverpudlian, Jimmy Melia from the Brighton camp. Jimmy eventually came on the line and, in the understandable heat of the moment, started talking up Brighton's prospects at Wembley. As Jimmy burbled on about conquering Europe next season, Ron winked at me and said, 'Jim, the only way you'll get into Europe is if you write a song!' Game, set and match – typical of Ron Atkinson's quick wit. He was always good for a line in those days. Just after I interviewed him one day for *Sports Report*, Ron Saunders, his opposite managerial number, bumped into us in the dressing-room corridor. Saunders, a man with a dry, understated wit, said, 'Hello, Ron, still telling them porkies?' to be met with the instant response, 'Yes, I was just saying what a good manager you are!'

Ron Atkinson remained good for a quote throughout his managerial career, but even he would yield to Brian Clough in such matters. In recent years, as the task of securing interviews for *Sports Report* has become more fraught, I have at times ruminated, 'Bloody hell, I used to take this nonsense from Cloughie, but at least he was worth it!' Brian Clough was the most infuriating, challenging, entertaining and charismatic character I have encountered in sport, never mind football, and the task of coaxing him on to *Sports Report* at various stages brought me a few grey hairs and dodgy moments. When I became the Midlands' football reporter in 1981, I was determined to get Cloughie on *Sports Report* more often. In his days with Derby, he was often on the programme, the usual mix of bombast and illuminating charm, but after settling in at Nottingham Forest and racking up an impressive tally of trophies, he went all monastic on the media, rationing his comments to a lucrative column in various tabloids. 'I've spent more bloody time with you lot than with my players,' he used to rasp. 'My wife Barbara is much more intelligent than me and she says I should do my job, shut up afterwards and go home. She's right.' Yet Cloughie loved to be asked, as you'd expect from someone who'd warm you with that blastfurnace of an ego. So I kept asking, in the process evolving from 'Who the hell are you?' to 'Thank you for asking, Patrick – but no', finally attaining the sunny uplands of 'Give me a ring on Friday, I'll let you know.' Finally, in December 1986, I cracked it and he obliged, for the first time in five years on *Sports Report*. Not without a fair degree of angst on the reporter's part, though. I had rung him the day before, passing a few pleasant minutes talking cricket, telling him I was off to Australia on the Sunday to cover the Ashes series, and letting slip the fact that I'd be at the City Ground on the morrow for the game against Manchester City. Cloughie then informed me 'You'll want me on your programme tomorrow then, young man.' For a scintilla of a second, I toyed with the ultimate put-down – 'I don't think so, Brian, we're pretty full tomorrow night' – decided I still wanted a career in radio sport and he agreed to come on, whatever the result. Just so I had no doubts that I was getting a big favour, Cloughie left me with the reassurance that 'It'll be an early Christmas present for you, Patrick – and tell those buggers in your London studio to give us some time for the interview.'

The information was duly imparted to a grateful editor and I presented myself at the City ground next day. Unfortunately my equanimity was disturbed by regular mentions throughout the afternoon that the great Brian Clough would be appearing on *Sports Report*, and be sure to stay tuned. The presenter at that time was occasionally guilty of the adjectival excesses we now associate with Sky Sports and he spared no hype in the build-up. At various stages throughout the match, journalistic colleagues would sidle up to me and express doubts that Cloughie would go through with it, unless we were paying him a hefty wedge. In vain did I protest that we weren't paying a penny and that Brian had always kept his word when he said he'd do an interview. I duly presented myself at the interview room just before five o'clock, convinced that the man who never wore a watch and assumed punctuality was for lesser mortals would stroll in some time over the next hour. The door burst open bang on five o'clock and there was Cloughie, holding two large tumblers of Scotch, demanding to do the interview immediately. I was constrained to point out that James Alexander Gordon was just clearing his throat to deliver the results and could he hang on for just five minutes? Grudgingly, he accepted the point that even Brian Clough has to wait for the football results, and proceeded to harangue me with his views on England's cricketing deficiencies in Australia. As he warmed to his task, Brian relieved me of the generous beaker of Scotch I had been cradling. There was a reason for that – he'd already polished off his. As the producer informed me down the line that they were breaking with precedent and starting off the football section with Cloughie live, rather than going around the grounds for reports, I looked across at my interviewee and felt a chill. Brian had supped well, rather than wisely, before he had presented himself for the interview. It was common knowledge around that time that occasionally Cloughie had a tincture or two to get him through the strains of match day. This afternoon was one of them. As I heard the producer say down the line 'Coming to you in ten seconds', I realised I'd forgotten to tell Brian the interview was live, that the usual flow of salty language with which he peppered recorded interviews would be unappreciated this time. What followed remained the longest eight minutes of my life.

Straight away, he threw me by asking what were the other scores involving sides who, like Forest, were near the top of the table. Mercifully I could remember them and I had passed his first test. Those piercing hazel eyes were a tad rheumy after the afternoon's activities, but they still followed me, teasing and challenging. After I'd summarised his trenchant views on Margaret Thatcher and her attitude to football, he rewarded me with a terse 'Haven't I just bloody said that?', and punished me with a couple of short answers. He warmed to his theme when he started talking about his son, Nigel, who had just broken into the Forest first team – the first time he'd commented publicly on that, much to the pleasure of the sceptical hacks listening in the press box, with pens poised. By now, I was praying that Brian wouldn't push us over the parapet of good taste, as the interview passed through an unparalleled duration for *Sports Report*. As the perspiration flowed down both sides of my face, and Brian looked sadly as his second empty tumbler, I thanked him for his time, only to receive the cheery riposte 'You come back from Australia a little more talented.' Typical Clough: he'd never let you relax, always ready to take you down a notch or two, second-guessing your best efforts. Yet he'd praise at the most surprising times. In the late 1980s, I had been so taken by the style and vibrancy of Forest's 4–1 defeat of Coventry City that I offered the opinion on *Sports Report* that 'Forest are the kind of team to take your granny to watch.' As I supped my pint afterwards in the Jubilee Club at the City ground, I was summoned to his imperial presence. In front of several members of his staff and family friends, he thanked me warmly, poured a large brandy and chatted amiably about cricket for another hour. If you had any sense, you never talked football with Cloughie – he'd only ask 'What do you know about it?'

I still miss the old boy in professional terms. He brightened up many a dull day, something we'll never be able to say about many current managers who'll fill the requisite three minutes on *Sports Report*, but offer nothing that's illuminating. You can't expect much from someone who's been so involved so recently in a match, but there are some beacons of individualism – Gordon Strachan, Graeme Souness, Peter Reid and Martin O'Neill for instance. Our programme tends to get ready co-operation from such characters, because they've grown up with us, as young players, then seasoned internationals and now managers. When *Sports Report* celebrated its fortieth birthday in January 1988, Graham Taylor, at the time Aston Villa's manager, was so pleased to be asked to come live on to the programme that he asked if he had time first to ring his father to tell him to listen. I'm not so sure we have the same respect from the current crop of players. They seem inordinately fond of television, perhaps because it's such an attractive vehicle for their latest range of leisurewear or because the interviewers are hardly Paxmanesque, as they are asked how pleased they are at scoring a goal – also known as doing their job. Never mind, the programme will be there long after Alex Ferguson has cowed an inquisitor for the last time. You only need to listen to the car radios after a game as they inch their way through the traffic. Spare a thought for the reporters next time you hear that stirring signature tune at five o'clock. Someone will be shouting despairingly at no one in particular, 'Oh my God, is it that time already?' Odds on it'll be me.

MICHAEL PARKINSON

The Lancashire Poet

*Journalist and broadcaster Michael Parkinson
received his footballing education at Barnsley FC
in the days of George Robledo, Danny
Blanchflower and the wonderful Sidney 'Skinner'
Normanton.*

The 50th anniversary of *Sports Report*. 'Te-tum, te-tum, te-tum, te-tum; te-tiddly-tum, te-tum'. You know the one. Listening to the echoes of forgotten years, there is one distinct voice. It belonged to H. D. 'Donny' Davies, 'Old International' of the *Manchester Guardian*, who was one of eight football writers to perish in the Munich disaster of 1958.

Davies was once described by Neville Cardus as 'very much a Lancashire poet'. He inspired a generation of young journalists by proving it was possible to create literature out of reporting a sporting event. No matter how good he was on the page – and you could smell Old Trafford when he described it – the addition of his voice brought the prose to life. Then you could touch the crowd, hear the jokes, taste the hot pot. His discursions were as lively as his descriptions. Once, reporting a marvellous display of dribbling by a Bolton Wanderers player at Burnden Park, he recalled the heckler at a political meeting asking a know-all MP: 'Has tha' ivver had DTs?' The politician was affronted. 'Never,' he said. 'Well, then, tha's seen nowt,' said the heckler. Reporting on a scrappy game between Manchester United and Stoke, he told his listeners on *Sports Report*: 'This game at times reminded

me of the Oxford undergraduate who took his mother to see a
soccer match for the very first time. 'What is the object of this
game, Archie dear?' she asked. 'To kick the ball between the
posts,' said Archie. 'But', the lady continued, 'wouldn't it be
simpler if they all got out of each other's way?'

Davies once described his contribution to *Sports Report* as 'a
three-minute jumble of fact and comment'. He was a modest man.
Even today, nearly 50 years hence and read as prose without the
benefit of his distinctive Bolton accent, they are perfect vignettes
of the reporter's craft. Recalling them set me wondering if Davies
would find employment on today's programme or if he might be
considered altogether too whimsical and old-fashioned. Similarly,
while listening to *Test Match Special* celebrating its 40th birthday
and a singular contribution to the better understanding of cricket,
I speculated on what chance a young John Arlott might have of
making the team. The day of the poet-commentator appears to be
over. There are not many of them around nowadays. It could be
said there never were, which is what made them special.

It seems to me that a new-style commentator has emerged. He is
either a former professional with a necessarily analytical technique
or a gung-ho broadcaster of the modern school, representing what
might be termed the fanzine method of match reporting. I am not
bemoaning the presence of former players who have used their
experience to pick the lock of our ignorance. What is missing is that
counter-balancing opinion of the layman, particularly if, like
Davies and Arlott, their deep love and knowledge of games are
underpinned by both intellect and humour. Their value is not
simply the vocabulary they bring to the job but the sense that for all
sport is important, it is a pastime best considered as a hobby rather
than a profession. Such an observation would not have raised an
eyebrow when Arlott and Davies began their careers. Nowadays,
any suggestion that sport is not a business can be dismissed as
romantic piffle and you could argue that sport has more need than
ever of an opinion which brings it firmly back to earth. I call as
evidence a report by Donny Davies from Maine Road when the
performance of a City player proved too much for a fan on the
terraces. 'Look at him trying to dribble,' he yelled. 'Why doesn't he
learn? After all, he's got nothing else to do.' Precisely.

CLARE BALDING

Frankie's Magnificent Seven

*A member of a distinguished racing family and a
champion amateur rider, Clare Balding has
reported on equestrian events of all kinds for both
BBC television and radio. She is also a regular
member of Radio Five Live's Wimbledon
commentary team.*

Saturday 28 September 1996 was a typically busy Saturday of
Sport: the Old Firm Derby at Ibrox was the commentary match
on 5 Live, and, with half a dozen Premiership matches as well,
racing at Ascot was halfway down the running order for the
afternoon. It was the first day of the 'Festival of Racing': seven
good, competitive races with the Queen Elizabeth II stakes as
the highlight, one of the year's most valuable and prestigious
mile contests.

Peter Bromley, our distinguished racing correspondent and
commentator, did the usual preview, looking ahead to the big
race and discussing the merits of the main contenders:
Godolphin's Mark of Esteem, the French trained Ashkalani,
and Bosra Sham, the best filly in the country.

The current talking-point in racing was the accident a week
before at Newbury. Willie Carson had suffered horrific injuries
in the paddock when he was kicked by a filly and was taken to
hospital with a lacerated liver. He would live, but his future as

a jockey was in doubt, and racing journalists made it clear they thought he was a fool to even think of a comeback. The dangers of race riding had once more been highlighted, and one of the most popular and well known faces of the weighing-room was in intensive care.

Little did we know that by the next morning, racing would be the front-page lead in all the newspapers for the right reasons, that people up and down the land would be talking about another jockey, about the extraordinary achievement of a bubbly little Italian. He had a wonderful gift: he could not only make a Ford Capri of a racehorse run like a Ferrari, but he enjoyed it – no, loved it! Grinning from ear to ear after every winner, leaping from their backs like a human jack in the box, exploding with enthusiasm for the sport, Frankie Dettori was the best thing that had happened to racing since the days of Piggott and Carson at their best.

Dettori had missed a large chunk of the summer with a broken elbow and had spent Royal Ascot on the sidelines, trying his hand as a TV pundit and making it look easy. Now he was back at the course in more familiar clothes – silks and white breeches, with a crash cap replacing the top hat. He had a ride in all seven races on that afternoon, some of them fancied, others not.

His low crouching drive took Wall Street to a workmanlike victory in the first and got the better of a three-way photograph on Diffident in the second race, by a short head. The afternoon had started well and he was more than willing to give an interview before the QE2 (as it's known) to talk about Mark of Esteem's chances. He had been thinking about the race for the last couple of days, and was nervous because he knew how important it was for the horse to win this to prove himself a champion. Being superstitious, he was also worried that he might have used up all his luck by winning the first two races!

Frankie rode the text-book race, waiting until the furlong marker to make his move and accelerating with a turbo boost to pass Bosra Sham. He came in to a wonderful reception, and despite being asked by an official if he would mind not doing his flying leap, went ahead when he saw Sheikh Mohammed looking perplexed – Godolphin had won the first three races, Mark of Esteem had proved himself the best miler in Europe, there was plenty to celebrate. After all, when Sheikh Mohammed says 'jump', you jump.

We talked to Simon Crisford, the Godolphin racing manager, about Mark of Esteem, who at this stage of the afternoon was the equine star. I thought I'd wait until after the 4th race to interview Frankie, because he was busy with television and I didn't want to rush it. There were 26 runners in the Tote Festival Handicap and, although he had a good chance on Decorated Hero, he was badly drawn. He came from way off the pace to win at 7–1 for his principal trainer and mentor, John Gosden. Holding up his hand to signify '4 out of 4', he was bubbling.

'When a jockey's confidence is high, horses can feel it,' he said, 'What a day!'

Joanne Watson, the producer of *Sport on Five*, had more foresight than the rest of us, and told the engineers not to start de-rigging the commentary equipment, just in case. Peter Bromley was scribbling away at his piece, and as we watched the monitor in the little control room Fatefully battled to beat 17 other runners in the 5th race, with Dettori in the saddle again.

'You might have to wait to file that piece,' our producer Rob Smith suggested to Peter, 'if Frankie wins the next you'll have to change that 5-timer to 6.'

Three jockeys had ridden all six winners on the card before – Alec Russell, Sir Gordon Richards and, most recently, Willie Carson in 1990, but never had it been done on such a competitive day. *Sport on Five* was into second-half commentary on Rangers v Celtic, so we told them just to keep an eye on the racing, and we would send the piece later.

Dettori was riding a two-year-old filly called Lochangel in the 6th race, trained by my father, Ian Balding. He was in a dreadful state, terrified of letting Frankie down if she didn't win and talking down her chances, despite the fact that she had shown bags of natural speed and was a half-sister to the sprinter Lochsong with whom he and Frankie had enjoyed such success.

Lochangel looked surprised at the sheer numbers of people gathered around the paddock to wish Frankie well – she was not used to such attention. The orders were to come from off the pace and hope she would quicken up. She popped out of the stalls, ears pricked, and made all the running.

'Sometimes you have to improvise,' said Frankie. 'The instructions went out the window!'

That is the difference between a good jockey and a great one. He could assess a situation in a split second and had the confidence to change the plan if necessary. With this little bit of brilliance, he had equalled the record. He was presented with a magnum of champagne in the winner's enclosure, thanked the crowd for their support and celebrated his bit of history. It was almost bang on 5 o'clock and Ian Payne read out 'Frankie's had 5 out of 5, no make that 6' in the *Sports Report* headlines. Joanne Watson agreed that we would take commentary on the last race.

Peter Bromley has always maintained that the secret of his longevity is leaving before the last race to beat the traffic. He can often be seen bolting for the car park as soon as he has filed his voicepiece, lumping his huge case with him before the mad dash after the last. This time he was happy to stay. The 20,000 spectators all remained, only the odd bookmaker ducking for cover. Dettori was on board an unpredictable horse called Fujiyama Crest who was quoted at 12–1 in the morning papers. His trainer Michael Stoute said the horse couldn't possibly win.

By the time Dettori walked out to the paddock to climb on board, the sheer weight of expectation, hope and goodwill had forced the odds in to 2–1 favourite. Frankie said afterwards that when he saw the electronic betting board, he just couldn't believe it.

At 5.35, *Sports Report* played the package summing up Dettori's day so far. Peter picked up off the back of it for the last half mile of the race. Frankie and Fujiyama Crest had set out to make the running for the full two miles of the long-distance handicap. The bell went as the field turned into the straight, he was still in front and the crowd realised that they were about to witness history. A huge roar went up, and as one of those lucky enough to have been in the stands, I could swear that the noise literally carried the horse to the line.

Bromley gave his all in a memorable commentary, his rumbling voice reaching a crescendo: 'They're into the last furlong, and I don't think you'll hear a word I'm saying because you'll realise that Fujiyama Crest and Frankie Dettori have the lead, but Northern Fleet is going after him... Fujiyama Crest has won it.' He bellowed, 'Frankie Dettori's Seven. That is history made, the crowd are running towards the unsaddling enclosure to greet today's hero – Frankie Dettori!'

A mad rush to the winner's enclosure was rewarded by the sight of normally reserved men hugging each other, Dettori screaming with delight and holding up his fingers in disbelief to signify SEVEN!! Cynical journalists with tears in their eyes, people cheering and clapping, just thrilled that they had been there to see it. Frankie hugged the horse and gave his second leap of the afternoon – twice as high as the first and flapping his arms on the way down. He leapt on Michael Stoute, hugging him like a giant teddy bear.

He applauded the crowd who, 30 deep, surrounded the amphitheatre of an enclosure, all straining to see him. It was Wembley on Cup final day, Centre Court at Wimbledon, the 18th green at St Andrew's, and the boxing ring in Las Vegas all rolled into one. A cauldron of excitement and pleasure. The atmosphere was extraordinary as lovers of the sport, and those with a passing interest, realised that this would never be equalled, not on such a competitive day of racing, not at Ascot, not like this.

Another magnum of champagne appeared, this time sprayed over everyone as he ran round and round the winner's enclosure. Frankie found out that Arsenal had beaten Sunderland – an ardent fan, his day was complete.

'Don't touch me, I'm red 'ot! I'm gonna do the Lottery tonight, I tell ya!' he laughed in his half-Italian, half-cockney accent, 'Whatta day. I've had some great days in my life but this will take some beating – it's incredible. I'd like to thank all my supporters, and all the people here. It's been a dream come true.'

It made the news bulletins that night, and was the front-page lead in all the morning's papers, as they recognised what was undoubtedly one of the greatest ever sporting achievements. A Magnificent Seven that paid out at odds of 25,095–1 for the few lucky enough to combine all of his mounts in an accumulated bet. Smaller bookmakers were put out of business, the larger ones estimated that they had lost £25 to £30 million.

It took a while for the enormity of what he had done to sink in, but later Frankie reflected with characteristic humility. 'It might look as though it was my day, but for me it was horse racing's day. The people's day. An occasion to show that a day at the races can be as much fun as any football match, tennis final or golf tournament.'

Who could ask for a better advertisement for racing? Who could ask for a better day of sport?

DON MOSEY

In Memoriam Brian Johnston

Brian Johnston, the mainstay of Test Match
Special *for over 20 years and one of the most
familiar voices on radio, died on 5 January 1994.
This tribute by his friend and* TMS *colleague Don
Mosey was broadcast on* Sports Report *three days
later.*

Quite simply, Brian Johnston refused to grow old. He did not
so much fight the ageing process as ignore it – it simply didn't
exist. His theme in life was fun and laughter – he left a legacy of
laughter all over the world, and what a wickedly infectious
form of laughter it was.

For 18 summers on *Test Match Special* we played a pencil-
and-paper word game. The idea was to build up words from
letters we gave each other – a relic I suspect of the days when he
was under-employed in the office of the family business. I once
calculated that we'd played nearly 2,000 games and during one
of them I slipped him – much to his surprise – the letter 'J'. It was
not helpful. He hesitated, and then started to chuckle. Two
minutes later, the eight people in the commentary box were
shaking with hysterical laughter, and not one of them knew
why. To this day, ten or twelve years later, I can't address myself
to the letter 'J' without beginning to smile – I should have fun
dating letters this month.

We were an odd couple I suppose, totally different in background, but we got on rather nicely. Between cricket seasons we had a regular correspondence to and from wherever we happened to be in the world. It did not always proceed smoothly because Brian invariably travelled without his address book, and thus I used to receive cards inscribed:

> The Alderman,
> Sorry I've Forgotten His Address,
> Morecambe,
> Lancs,
> England

and after that

> The Alderman,
> Sorry I've Forgotten It Again
> etc.

Now, all these reached me, which is quite remarkable when you remember that Brian's handwriting could only be deciphered by his immediate family, or by a dispensing chemist.

We all at one time or another fell victims to his practical jokes – no one escaped. He sent, or caused his publishers to send, a book to our mutual friend F. S. Trueman addressed to 'Sir Frederick Trueman', which caused Fred's local postman to beat the door and gasp: 'Eee I'm right pleased tha's got th' knighthood at last Fred,' and he actually conned me into attempting to sing a duet with Ian Wallace, the operatic bass baritone, in the middle of *Test Match Special*. That was on Radio 3, no less, and I think it set the Music Programme back about thirty years.

Brian would have loved to be a professional entertainer of another sort – ideally, he would have been a seventh member of the Crazy Gang at the Victoria Palace – and he loved pantomime. Not too long ago, he actually signed up to play Alderman Fitzwarren in a Christmas production of *Dick Whittington* in Bournemouth I think, but sadly it fell through before he got on stage. Can't you just imagine – 'Oh Whitters old man I understand you want to marry my daughter – and my, what a handsome moggy you've got there.'

Brian, John Paul Getty and myself – and there's a trio to conjure with – were, I suppose, the senior echelon of the *Neighbours* fan club in the United Kingdom, and when two members of the cast of the Australian soap opera – Madge and Harold – came over to play in a panto, in of all the unlikely places, Stockport, Brian insisted that we go, dragging along a pair of mystified and head-shaking wives to see it. He joined in every raucous chorus and bellowed advice like 'Look out – he's behind you' with all the other five- to ten-year-olds in the Davenport Theatre, and then we took Madge and Harold out to dinner.

He collected excruciatingly vulgar seaside postcards – you know the sort of thing, huge fat ladies and weedy hen-pecked husbands and willowy blondes with outstanding pneumatic charms – to send to all the most pompous people he knew – and he knew quite a lot of them. And everyone had to have a nickname – although I never, incidentally, called him Johnners. But to him, quite suddenly and unexpectedly in mid-commentary one day, I became 'The Alderman', and do you know, he could not for the life of him remember why he came to call me that.

But all this was only half the man. Brian was kind, gentle, generous. He was caring, compassionate and concerned. In all the years I worked with him, I never heard him utter an unkind or uncharitable word about anyone. He was a dear man, a lovely human being. I'm so glad, so very glad, to have known him.

IAN PAYNE AND GILL PULSFORD

Sports Report Now

Ian Payne and Gill Pulsford are the current incumbents of the Sports Report *hot seats, now in their fourth season. Ian is an experienced all-round reporter with an ear for the offbeat and an eye for the unusual, while Gill is a long-serving and highly-respected producer who also masterminds BBC Radio's motor sport coverage.*

Three things have changed since *Sports Report* went on the air in 1948:

1. There is more sport.
2. Everything is faster.
3. There is more competition.

When *Sports Report* began, there was no real competition at all. The only other way you could get hold of the football results on a Saturday evening was by waiting for the evening newspaper to come out. 14 million people tuned in; today it is around a million. Despite all the other options for the listener, this is still the biggest radio audience on Saturday afternoon.

Listening to some of the early broadcasts you notice how much more deliberate everything was. Today there is so much more information to give, and so many more rivals to try and outdo with the speed of the service. There is also a much greater emphasis on getting immediate reaction from players and managers these days. Fifty years ago a match report would suffice – and that would often be delivered by a reporter who had travelled back from, say, Highbury, in a taxi to the studios in Broadcasting House. A discussion would often follow, with several notable men (always men) of the day giving their various opinions. Today, if you don't hear from the protagonists, you haven't heard the full story.

Basically, though, *Sports Report* remains the same in many ways. The most comprehensive and up to date coverage of sport throughout the world every Saturday evening. We only hope it stays as such for the next fifty years.

Like so many weekly programmes, it all begins with a planning meeting on Monday. We look at the diary and in particular the football fixture list. Our first priority is to decide whether the commentary match (which has usually already been selected) is the right one. We will usually pick the biggest game of the afternoon. If it is Manchester United against Liverpool, it is an easy decision to make, but sometimes there are three equally important games. That is when you have to weigh up all sorts of things – where are the teams in the table, are there any local derbies, is it about time we had a commentary on, say, Wimbledon, and which will generate the most crowd noise?

We then decide what preview features we need. These will usually entail a look ahead to games by focusing on various teams/players/managers/kitmen/fans … and it's not just the big teams. If an unlikely side is leading one of the lower divisions we might do something on them. Or if, for example, a club like Brighton is struggling and could even go out of business we would do something on them and perhaps send a reporter to the game. We always send reporters to every Premiership match, plus a top Scottish match and at least one from the Football League.

We also plan our coverage of other sports on Monday. There might be a rugby union international, or a rugby league game in the Challenge Cup. We always cover racing and the programme from Aintree for the Grand National in 1997 was particularly interesting.

If something big happens during the week, we can change our plans accordingly. When Juninho signed for Middlesbrough, we changed our commentary game just a day before the match.

Wednesday evening matches now play an important role during the football season. There is almost always a story coming from one of the top mid-week games and with so many British clubs in Europe, and doing well, we often plan our previews after Wednesday night.

Thursdays and Fridays are spent putting the finishing touches to the planning. There may be taped features to record and we can spend several hours in the studio putting them together.

Saturday morning is usually spent writing the final scripts and recording the opening of the programme with music, then it is down to the studio at about 12.40 p.m., with Sport on Five on the air at one o'clock – previews of the events from all the reporters, live interviews and taped features with managers and players, football team news at 2.40pm, and from kick-off at three o'clock, live action all the way.

At five o'clock it's time for Sport Report ... a famous phrase, followed by even more famous music. It will probably never be changed and it is a decision that is never questioned. We may change many things, but that signature tune will probably be with us for as long as the programme remains on the air.

The football results are read, as always, by James Alexander Gordon, and then there are reports from all our featured games. As this is all going on, the studio producer is listening out for any reporter who might call out 'I've got Mr X here with me now for a live interview,' and we go to them.

Live interviews are often a step into the unknown. You never know what the interviewee is going to say – especially immediately after a match when emotions run high. Some managers are co-operative to a point above and beyond the call of duty. Both Peter Reid and Dave Bassett did live interviews immediately after their teams had been relegated, when they would have been forgiven for shutting themselves away with their sorrows. On the other hand, there are managers and players who one would think would be delighted to talk to their public but...

The well oiled machine hit the buffers in quite spectacular style on Saturday 21 December 1996. All the microphones in the main studio packed up. At the same time. Right in the middle of the programme. Pat Murphy was covering the first Test match between Zimbabwe and England in Bulawayo, and the producer got him to carry on presenting the programme from there, handing to Lee McKenzie at Ascot for a racing commentary and Nick Mullins at Sale for a spot of rugby union. Yes, the programme could be presented from Bulawayo, but not from the other side of the studio glass. The production team ended up in a tiny cupboard-like studio with engineers crawling all around, while Peter Drury was being alerted that he might well have to continue presenting the programme from Nottingham Forest v Arsenal once the football got underway. As usual, it didn't come to that. The engineers saved the day and the listeners wouldn't have noticed there were any problems. Much.

At six o'clock, everyone goes to the pub for a well earned drink. It can be fraught and frantic, but it is fun.

MAGIC MOMENTS...

Queen Elizabeth the Queen Mother, a distinguished supporter of National Hunt racing for many years, suffered an early demise at the hands of Peter Bromley during a commentary at Newbury. This is what Peter said:

'... and this is the Game Spirit Chase, named of course by Game Spirit, a lovely horse that was owned by Her Majesty the Queen Mother who dropped dead here after a very long and distinguished career...'.

ENDPIECE

In February 1959 Angus Mackay acknowledged the congratulations of the BBC Establishment on *Sports Report's* 'one thousandth' programme in the following terms. Who instituted this celebration is not known, but their grasp of arithmetic must have been somewhat shaky. Allowing for summer breaks, *Sports Report* must in reality have been approaching its five hundredth edition in February 1959.

THE BRITISH BROADCASTING CORPORATION
Broadcasting House, London, W.1

12th February 1959

Dear Rooney,

Many thanks for your note of congratulations on our One Thousandth programme. Eamonn and I did not realise that so much notice would be taken of this celebration programme but we much appreciate the good wishes which were sent to us.

Let's hope we and the programme last long enough to make it 2,000 in 1967 – an awful thought, isn't it?

Yours...

Angus Mackay

H. Rooney Pelletier
Controller, Programme Planning (Sound)
Broadcasting House

SPORTS REPORT
CHRONOLOGY

3 JANUARY 1948
First edition of *Sports Report* – 'a new Saturday feature for sportsmen'
Airtime: 5.30–6.00pm on the Light Programme
Signature tune: 'Out of the Blue' by Hubert Bath
Presenter: Raymond Glendenning
Producer: Angus Mackay

20 AUGUST 1955
Airtime: 5.00–6.00pm on the Light Programme
Sports Report extended to one hour in response to the new challenge from television and the need to get the football results on earlier
Presenter: Eamonn Andrews
Producer: Angus Mackay

7 FEBRUARY 1959
Advertised as 'the 1,000th edition of *Sports Report* in which Eamonn Andrews and Angus Mackay have worked together as narrator and producer'. As the programme had by then been running only 11 years, Angus's arithmetic would appear to be suspect!

25 APRIL 1964
Eamonn Andrew's last programme as presenter after 13 years

22 AUGUST 1964
Sports Report moves from the Light to the Third programme, following a 'Sports Service' consisting of live commentaries interspersed with classical and light music – a forerunner of *Sport on Five*
Presenter: Robin Marlar
Producer: Angus Mackay

30 SEPTEMBER 1967
Introduction of the BBC's 'Swinging New Radio Service' – four radio networks, including the new Radio One
Sports Report on Radio Three

4 APRIL 1970
First edition of *Sport on Two*, replacing the Radio Three Sports Service
Airtime 2.30pm–6.00pm, including *Sports Report*
Presenter: Peter Jones
Producers: Jacob de Vries and Angus Mackay

29 APRIL 1972
Angus Mackay's last edition as Producer of *Sports Report* after 24 years
Presenter: Desmond Lynam

6 JANUARY 1973
Sports Report's 25th birthday
Presenter: Peter Jones
Producer: Bob Burrows

7 JANUARY 1978
30th birthday edition of *Sports Report*
Presenter: Desmond Lynam

2 JANUARY 1988
40th anniversary edition of *Sports Report*
Presenter: Peter Jones (in dinner jacket)
Producer: Rob Hastie

1 SEPTEMBER 1990
Introduction of the new Radio Five network, carrying sport, children's and educational programmes
Sport on Two becomes, with impeccable logic, *Sport on Five*.
Airtime: 1.30pm–6.00pm including *Sports Report*
Presenter: John Inverdale

2 APRIL 1994
Introduction of the new Radio Five Live network – a 24-hour news and sport service. *Sport on Five* gains half and hour –
Airtime: 1.00pm–6.00pm including *Sports Report*
Presenter: John Inverdale